# THE FORCE AWAKENS

*Star Wars: The Force Awakens* arrived in theaters a decade after the prequel trilogy came to its close, with a new creative team now exploring the galaxy that George Lucas had created in 1977. The film, directed by J.J. Abrams and co-written by him and Lawrence Kasdan, launched the space fantasy into a brand-new era, and to a new generation of fans.

Released on December 18, 2015, *The Force Awakens* continued the epic Skywalker saga with a seventh episode, catching up with familiar faces from the original trilogy in a story set thirty years after the events of *Star Wars: Return of the Jedi*. However, the main focus would fall on a younger group of heroes as they faced the villainous threat of a foe even more ruthless than the Empire that had preceded it: the First Order!

As it had done throughout production of the prequel trilogy, *Star Wars Insider* interviewed the cast and creators behind the saga's next chapter, providing fans with fascinating coverage of the making of the movie.

---


**TITAN EDITORIAL**
**Editor** Christopher Cooper
**Contributors** Tricia Barr, Mark Newbold, Darren Scott, Jonathan Wilkins
**Group Editor** Jake Devine
**Senior Creative Editor** David Leach
**Lead Creative Editor** Phoebe Hedges
**Editor** Jonathan Wilkins
**Assistant Editors** Louis Yamani & Ibraheem Kazi
**Editorial Assistant** Holly Smith
**Art Director** Oz Browne
**Designers** Dan Bura, David Colderley & Matt Bookman
**Head of Production** Kevin Wooff
**Production Manager** Jackie Flook
**Production Controllers** Caterina Falqui & Kelly Fenlon
**Publicity Manager** Will O'Mullane
**Publicist** Julia Oprzondek
**Direct Market Sales Coordinator** Chief Stride
**Digital & Marketing Manager** Jo Teather
**Marketing Coordinator** Lauren Noding

**Sales & Circulation Manager** Steve Tothill
**Head of Rights** Rosanna Anness
**Rights Executive** Pauline Savouré
**Head Of Creative & Business Development** Duncan Baizley
**Publishing Directors** Ricky Claydon & John Dziewiatkowski
**Chief Operating Officer** Andrew Sumner
**Publishers** Vivian Cheung & Nick Landau

*Star Wars: The Force Awakens 10th Anniversary Special Edition* is published by Titan Magazines, a division of Titan Publishing Group Limited, 144 Southwark Street, London SE1 0UP

First Edition November 2025
**Printed in China**

For sale in the U.S., Canada, U.K., and Eire

ISBN: 9781787746732
Titan Authorized User. TCN 4884



A CIP catalogue record for this title is available from the British Library.
10 9 8 7 6 5 4 3 2 1

**DISTRIBUTION**
**U.S. Distribution:**
Penguin Random House
**U.K. Distribution:**
MacMillan Distribution
**Direct Sales Market:**
Diamond Comic Distributors
**General Inquiries:**
customerservice@titanpublishingusa.com

eucomply OÜ Pärnu mnt 139b-14 11317
Tallinn, Estonia
hello@eucompliancepartner.com
+3375690241.

**LUCASFILM EDITORIAL**
**Senior Editor** Brett Rector
**Editor** Jennifer Pooley
**Creative Director** Michael Siglain
**Art Director** Troy Alders
**Story Group** Leland Chee, Pablo Hidalgo, Kate Izquierdo
**Creative Art Manager** Phil Szostak
**Asset Management** Shahana Alam, Chris Argyropoulos, Allison Bird, Jackey Cabrera, Elinor De La Torre, Gabrielle Levenson, Nick Miano, Bryce Pinkos, Sarah Williams.

**Special Thanks:**
Ryan Jalernpan & Kevin Pearl

Disney · Lucasfilm

# CONTENTS

# "IT'S REAL. ALL OF IT."

Helming a *Star Wars* movie is a huge responsibility, and one that J.J. Abrams—the director who was given the gargantuan task of bringing the saga back to movie theaters following a ten-year absence—approached with absolute respect and a great deal of love.

"It's funny, but I remember the first time I saw the words *Star Wars*," Abrams said of his first brush with the galaxy far, far away. "It was in *Starlog* magazine. I remember seeing the words and saying them aloud. There was something about it that felt unusual, and that was before the film came out. But it stuck with me."

Abrams was just 11 years old when he saw *Star Wars: A New Hope* for the first time, and described the experience as "mind-expanding." It was a movie that fed into his burgeoning desire to make films and tell stories himself.

"It was full of heart and romanticism and optimism and comedy and incredible conflict, and certainly visual effects like I had never seen before," the director said. "It was such a great story of the underdog and told with such great imagination.

"When you look back at the original, it is unbelievable how much they got right," he continued. "Not just the story and the characters and the casting. Not just the design, not just the music. All of it. When you look at all of it, you realize how much was nailed. You don't know so much in that movie, like what the Empire wants or the possibility that Darth Vader is Luke's father, or that Leia is Luke's sister. All these things exist, but none are explicit. Yet, it has that sense that this world is real and exists and is expansive. It felt beautifully considered and wonderfully told. For me, as a kid, it bowled me over. It's a world I wanted to get back to immediately."

As destiny would have it, not only would Abrams achieve his childhood dream of becoming Hollywood filmmaker, but he was also given the keys to the *Millennium Falcon* and a mission to take audiences back to the galaxy far, far away.

01 The first teaser trailer for *Star Wars: The Force Awakens* featured this evocative image of a crashed Star Destroyer in its opening frames.

# *THE FORCE AWAKENS* By Numbers

**7** Versions of the BB-8 prop used in the movie

**12** Days to net $1 billion in worldwide ticket sales

**50** The soundtrack earned John Williams his 50th Oscar nomination

**88 seconds** First teaser trailer duration

**136 minutes** Running time

**$247,966,675** Opening weekend box-office gross

**$2,068,223,624** Worldwide box office gross

---

## Key Dates

**First day of principal photography:** May 16, 2014
**Final day of principal photography:** November 6, 2014
**Teaser Trailer released:** November 28, 2014
**Full Trailer released:** October 19, 2015
**Novelization published:** eBook December 18, 2015; Hardcover January 5, 2016
**U.S. premiere:** December 18, 2015
**Home Video release:** April 5, 2016

# THE BEGINNING OF THE END

## *STAR WARS: THE FORCE AWAKENS*

Introducing a new era of heroes and villains while rejoining the lives of much-loved characters from the original movies, *Star Wars: The Force Awakens* also marked the beginning of the final chapter in the Skywalker saga.

In kicking off another *Star Wars* trilogy, *The Force Awakens* took its place with *A New Hope* and *The Phantom Menace* in marking the start of an epic adventure. Those three beginnings—initiating the stories of Anakin, Luke, and Rey—form their own trilogy of sorts: a trio of opening episode films within the nine-movie Skywalker saga. Their similarities showcase the core nature of a *Star Wars* tale, while their differences highlight how the character arcs of the three leads take them each down a different path. The seeds planted in these opening films come into bloom as each trilogy progresses, and as each protagonist grows into the hero they were meant to be.

As trilogy openers, each film introduces the core characters in the three-story arc: the protagonist, their allies, and their adversaries. In *The Phantom Menace*, Anakin Skywalker meets Padmé and Obi-Wan Kenobi, as well as Palpatine, who will define his trilogy's tragedy. In *A New Hope*, Luke befriends Leia and Han, and is pursued by Darth Vader, the principals of the Skywalker family saga. In *The Force Awakens*, Rey and Finn work to return Poe's droid to the Resistance, and Rey twice repels Kylo Ren in the process. By the time the prequel trilogy concluded with *Star Wars: Revenge of the Sith* (2005), the broader scope of the tragic fall of the Galactic Republic that led to civil war and the defeat of Emperor Palpatine in *Star Wars: Return of the Jedi* (1983) had been fleshed out. The six movie arc tied Luke Skywalker and Leia Organa's journey to reclaim galactic control from the oppressive regime of the Empire to the pivotal choices made by their parents, Anakin Skywalker and Padmé Amidala, 20 years earlier. The next trilogy begins 30 years after *Return of the Jedi*, and builds on the consequences of the Rebellion's costly triumph.

*The Force Awakens* opened with a new tyrannical threat known as the First Order besieging the village Tuanul on the desert world of Jakku. The landing party is led by a shadowy figure, who evokes the imposing specter of *Star Wars* übervillain Darth Vader, formerly known as Jedi Knight Anakin Skywalker. Village elder, Lor San Tekka, who has discovered a piece of the map to find the location of the missing Luke Skywalker, is brought before the dark commander Kylo Ren as his stormtroopers burn the village and round up its inhabitants. As Ren demands San Tekka turn over the map, the conversation reveals the two know each other.

"The First Order rose from the dark side...you did not," San Tekka says, prompting Ren's threat to show him the dark side. "You may try, but you cannot deny the truth that is your family," Tekka responds. The script then reads: "Suddenly Kylo Ren raises his LIGHTSABER—IGNITES IT—PERPENDICULAR SMALLER BLADES AT THE HILT, A UNIQUE BUZZ—YELLOW/RED ENERGY, SPITTING SPARKS AND SMOKE—as he RIPS IT DOWN ACROSS SAN TEKKA!"

It is only as the movie unfolds that we understand why the mention of "family" leads to Lor San Tekka's sudden murder in a fit of Kylo Ren's rage.

## Forsaking a Name

Kylo Ren is revealed to be Ben Solo, son of former rebel general Han Solo and Rebel Alliance and Resistance leader Leia Organa. He's also the nephew of legendary Jedi Knight Luke Skywalker.

Ben Solo can trace his lineage to many important families of the Skywalker saga; he is also the grandson of Padmé Amidala and Anakin Skywalker. His mother kept the name of the Alderaan royal family that adopted her and were instrumental in the formation of the Rebel Alliance. Yet, her son shares the modest first name Jedi Master Obi-Wan Kenobi assumed for 20 years after the fall of the Republic to secretly guard Luke as the boy was raised by Owen and Beru Lars. And Ben also has his father's last name, which in *Solo: A Star Wars Story* (2018, co-written by *The Force Awakens* screenwriter Lawrence Kasdan with his son Jonathan) was revealed not to be a family name at all, but one randomly assigned to Han by an Imperial bureaucrat when he enlisted in the Imperial war machine to escape a desolate life on

01 Previous page: Kylo Ren (Adam Driver) and the forces of the First Order make their presence felt on Jakku.

02 Poe Dameron (Oscar Isaac) has no defense against Kylo Ren's invasive Force-powered interrogation.

03 Kylo Ren stalks Rey and Finn on the snowy surface of Starkiller Base.

03

Corellia. Like his grandfather Darth Vader, Kylo Ren has shed the name he used as a Jedi to take on a title meant to deny his former self and the baggage of his family history.

One out-of-universe assumption could be that Ben Solo was named in a patriarchal normative mindset, in which children take the surnames of their father. But perhaps, within the *Star Wars* galaxy, Solo is the name that carries the least amount of baggage. Organa, Amidala, and Skywalker each play an iconic role in turning the tide against the Sith's stranglehold on the galaxy, keeping the spark of hope burning in the darkest of times—imagine having to live up to that. The name Solo, by contrast, is one with a less weighty connection to the past.

Kylo Ren's propensity for tantrums might have left him clueless to the whereabouts of Luke except for Poe's rash reaction to San Tekka's execution. Poe's blaster shot at Ren introduces new Force powers to the *Star Wars* franchise when the dark student halts the bolt in mid-air. Poe is taken captive, but he has bought time for BB-8 to disappear into the expansive Jakku sandscape with the map. Eluding the First Order turns out to be the least of BB-8's problems though, as the resource-poor planet harbors many desperate scavengers.

While Kylo tortures Poe for information back on his Star Destroyer *Finalizer*, BB-8 is captured by a scavenger, Teedo. Luckily, that isn't the end of the droid's story: destined to be sold for scrap at Niima Outpost, BB-8's calls for help are heard by a young woman who lives a solitary life on a backwater planet, her life defined not by privileged birthright but rather the absence of family bonds.

04

## Destiny and Droids

In *Star Wars*, we learn much about our heroes from how they first interact with their droids. Young Anakin, scavenging parts in his owner's junkyard, built a protocol droid to make his mother's life as a slave easier. Shmi tells Jedi Master Qui-Gon Jinn that her son "knows nothing of greed," as he volunteers to risk his life in a podrace to help a Jedi and handmaiden he just met. Teenage Luke, by contrast, is a bored farmhand who wishes for adventures among the stars. Acquiring a pair of droids from Jawas, Luke treats them as little more than useful machinery—even after he sees the fateful hologram from Princess Leia. Rey too lives a monotonous life in the desert, but she is patient rather than restless in her wait for a family who will never return. Heeding a droid's cries for rescue, she immediately treats the spherical robot with dignity: giving directions to a destination, warning of other hazards along the way, offering him temporary shelter from the impending nightfall—at least until the morning, when Rey is insistent, "you go."

The droids follow our heroes as their adventures progress, too, and serve as points of view into their mythic adventures. Anakin's flaw is his familial attachment: his emotions towards missing his mother are the first steps along what becomes a much darker path. Although he apparently pays little mind to leaving C-3PO behind to help Shmi, Anakin readily teams up with R2-D2 for a brazen flight of an N-1 starfighter in the space battle over Naboo. Once his adventure begins, Luke has both C-3PO and R2-D2 with him on his journey from the farm to Mos Eisley to the escape from the Death Star. Like his father, Luke flies with R2-D2 into the Battle of Yavin and carries off an even more spectacular miracle shot.

Like Luke, Rey and BB-8 share their adventure from Niima Outpost to Han Solo's freighter to Takodana—where they become separated when Rey is captured in the droid's place, in service of Kylo Ren's quest for the map to the last Jedi. At Starkiller Base, Rey frees herself from captivity before reuniting with Finn, along with Han and Chewie, on the ground, while BB-8 joins the air battle with his original companion, Poe.

## Equal and Opposite Reactions

Since *A New Hope, Star Wars* movies have depicted mythic journeys linked together through a series of character introductions: Darth Vader's storming of the *Tantive IV* corvette leads to Princess Leia, who previously hands the Death Star plans to R2-D2, who takes C-3PO down to Tatooine, where they meet simple farm boy Luke Skywalker and hermit Ben Kenobi. Much like Episode IV, an astromech droid's persistence helps propel the hero of *The Force Awakens* on her adventure.

04 Rey (Daisy Ridley) with her new friend BB-8.

05 The trio of droids who have played a vital role in the unfolding Skywalker saga.

06

Once Rey saves BB-8 and straightens out his askew antenna, she tries to send him on his way. But she can't resist his little ball droid wiggle and plaintive beeps, resulting in the iconic shot of Rey and her new friend rolling next to her across a sand dune. This moment is the beginning of her finding the belonging she has longed for. Like Dorothy in *The Wizard of Oz* (1939), Rey encounters other people who will shape her journey, including Han Solo, who is less mentor than prospective father figure.While Kylo's introduction marks him out as the classic bully type, Rey reveals herself to be a character who opposes that kind of behavior. She doesn't simply denounce bullying, she pushes back against it: first with Teedo to save BB-8, then to defend BB-8 when she thinks Finn has stolen his master's jacket. The escaped stormtrooper Finn hasn't yet found his willpower to stand against the repressive regime that trained him, but he has discovered that, despite the First Order's indoctrination, he knows what they are doing is wrong. His chance encounter with Rey and her endless resolve allows Rey to begin to nurture a team—BB-8, Finn, and even the wayward Han Solo and his co-pilot Chewbacca—that will resist and protect.

As producer Kathleen Kennedy noted about the storytelling of the sequel trilogy at *Star Wars* Celebration Chicago, 2019, *Star Wars* works because it is timely. In the age of the internet, indoctrinated bullying goes hand-in-hand with systemic oppression.

Rey beseeches Finn to stay in the fight, but moments later learns through her first encounter with Luke's lightsaber

07

in the cellar of Maz's Castle how frightened even heroes can be. That doesn't stop her from trying to draw the troopers away from BB-8 so he can escape Takodana. Ultimately, her nemesis Kylo Ren sees the map and his father in her mind, and takes her prisoner.

At Starkiller Base, Rey faces further interrogation by the character set up at the beginning of the movie as the worst kind of bully: one who will invade your mind, force his will upon your body, and kill you when he doesn't get what he wants. Anyone who has tackled bullying knows that having the fortitude to stand up for yourself in those moments is a superpower. So, while Kylo's parents, Han and Leia, embark on a personal quest to try to save what remains of their son, Rey is on a solitary journey in which she chooses to push back. The hard won resilliance she'd learned during her life on Jakku, that she uses against Teedo to save BB-8, is to stand tall, because often the bully is more afraid than most.

Strapped to the interrogation chair, Rey proves the stronger of the two. Kylo thinks himself superior, but quickly finds otherwise. Rey isn't just powerful in the Force—she is strong enough to learn Kylo's deepest fear. "You're afraid," she hurls at him, "that you'll never be as strong as Darth Vader." She is defenseless, yet Kylo Ren flees the room and Rey escapes. It is not until Kylo kills his father, Han, and maims her friend, Finn, that Rey reaches for the lightsaber once held by Luke and his father Anakin before him. Now is her time to continue the legacy of Padmé Amidala and Leia Organa to resist when others cannot.

06 Rey with potential mentor Han Solo (Harrison Ford).

07 In the depths of Maz Kanata's castle, Rey is drawn to a chest containing Luke Skywalker's old lightsaber.

# DESTINY'S CHILD

## DAISY RIDLEY: REY

Abandoned by her parents on the unforgiving planet Jakku, Rey was forced to spend her childhood fending for herself. Exchanging scavenged scrap for food portions, she always clung to the hope that her parents would return, until an unexpected encounter with a lost droid took her to the stars.

he first thing Daisy Ridley heard about a new *Star Wars* movie being made was when some friends mentioned it in passing. "I don't know why; I just had this weird feeling," the actor told *Star Wars Insider* in 2015. "I immediately emailed my agent and said that I needed to be seen for it, and I wound up getting an audition."

Given the stakes of securing a role in one of cinema's most enduring franchises were understandably high, Ridley arrived for her first audition an hour early. "I was literally pacing up and down outside. I'd never been nervous like that before," she said. "But it was the first time in any audition process that I'd felt everyone was rooting for, if not for me, then the idea of an unknown actor getting the part."

Ridley admitted that before securing the role of Rey, the lead protagonist in *Star Wars: The Force Awakens'* impressive ensemble cast, she'd had no idea that her part would be so central to the new trilogy. "I knew it was a big part, but I didn't know that it would be the lead," she revealed. "I didn't know what Rey's journey would be and where she would end up. It was only when I read the script that I realized the enormity of the part."

As seemingly inescapable as the *Star Wars* phenomenon has been since 1977, the space fantasy hadn't impacted much upon Ridley's life until she was cast in the movie. "Because I'm younger than the first generation of *Star Wars* fans, it wasn't such a huge thing [for me]. I do remember being in the cinema [when I was young] and watching one of the films, and being terrified," she laughed. "*Star Wars* does permeate popular culture; It's on magazine covers, it's referenced everywhere, but it was only this year that it became a really big part of my life," she added.

That said, the impact of acting in famous *Star Wars* environments, like the main hold and cockpit of the *Millennium Falcon*, were not lost on Ridley. "It was such an iconic set and the director, J.J. Abrams, really wanted it to be perfect, so there was no mistaking what we were trying to create," said Ridley. "There were moments where I was, like, '*I'm* flying the *Millennium Falcon*!'"

Principal photography on the movie began on May 16, 2014, on location in Abu Dhabi, which doubled for the wreckage-strewn desert planet Jakku. Ridley and co-star John Boyega arrived a few days before cameras rolled in order to acclimatize to the region's stifling temperatures. "It was so hot that you could literally feel the sand burning through your shoes," Ridley recalled. "But, once you gave in to the heat, it was okay. You knew it was consistent; it wasn't going to change, so there was no point in fighting it."

02

01 Previous page: Daisy Ridley as Rey.

02 Adam Driver (Kylo Ren) and Daisy Ridley (Rey) during filming of their lightsaber duel.

03 John Boyega (center) and Ridley (right) during fight training.

04 Ridley said filming on the *Millennium Falcon* set was a "moment."

05 Rey (Ridley) and Finn (Boyega) attempt to escape the First Order on Jakku.

Even so, filming chase scenes as Rey, Finn, and BB-8 try to evade capture by the First Order tested the mettle of both performers. "When it got to the scenes where we had to run, the mix of hard and soft sand was the hardest part. That was a killer on the legs," Ridley confessed. "We'd go from doing lots of stunt things to acting and intimate moments, so towards the end of Abu Dhabi, I looked back and thought, 'I've really come a long way since the beginning. I could do the first few days again.'"

Despite sharing several scenes with Boyega, Ridley felt their on (and off)-screen chemistry really came into its own when the production set up shop at Pinewood Studios in England. "John became like an annoying little brother," she joked. "He was always telling me to shut up because I sing *all* the time! That relationship wasn't there at first, but once we started filming in London, and building that relationship through the scenes, it was easy. It's a chemistry thing that's not hard to find with someone you get on with. We're both incredibly silly, and you could feel the adults on set thinking, 'Oh, we've got two children here!'"

Another actor that Ridley shared several important scenes with in *The Force Awakens* was screen legend Harrison Ford, who reprised his original trilogy role of Han Solo—just one of several *Star Wars* veterans who returned for the new film.

"When I first met Harrison Ford, we just sat down for a coffee together," said Ridley. "He was talking about his experience in the whole thing, not just as Han Solo, but the *Star Wars* saga. Then we all had dinner together, which was great. The people who came back [for this film] are like a family, so I feel honored that I've been allowed to continue the journey [with them]."

03

04

05

The theme of found family runs strong in *Star Wars* storytelling, and Ridley saw comparisons between the connections on set and those her character forms during the movie's plot. "It felt like a family," she confirmed. "It's that feeling of bonding. Rey is trying to find her place in the galaxy in the same way that I was trying to find my place in this world. I felt so welcomed and taken in, and people seemed to care how I felt, which translated into the Rey thing as well. She suddenly has these people who care about her. The similarities were really nice."

# ROGUE TROOPER

## JOHN BOYEGA: FINN

Trained as a First Order stormtrooper since birth, FN-2187 was committed to the regime's mission until orders to commit a massacre on Jakku sparked a fire in his conscience. Given the name Finn by Resistance pilot Poe Dameron as the duo fought to escape a Star Destroyer, the former found a new cause to fight for.

"Finn is definitely the physical representation of the young generation when it comes to the *Star Wars* galaxy," actor John Boyega told *Insider* about his role as an ex-stormtrooper in *The Force Awakens*. "*Star Wars* has a huge following, but there is a small percentage of young people who haven't been introduced to that galaxy, or don't know how to relate to the movies. Finn is their direct link. He doesn't know what's going on and is freaked out by droids and aliens. I think the audience will enjoy a relatable character and his experiences."

Boyega went through seven months of auditions before learning that he'd been cast as Finn, including a screen test with Chewbacca. "From the get-go, they specified that it was a male leading role," he revealed. "*Star Wars* is an ensemble cast, so we have lots of leads that create the narrative, and I didn't know that Finn was so central to the story. I only found that out halfway through the audition process when J.J. Abrams said, 'You're the guy. You know that, right?' I was like, 'Ahh! Okay, it's time to get the acting chops together and do something!'"

His casting was finally confirmed over a cup of tea. "I got an email from J.J. asking where I was and if I could get to a little café in Mayfair, London," Boyega relates. "I hopped in a cab, drove down, and found J.J. drinking a cup of tea. We had a brief conversation, and he asked me whether I was ready. Then, he told me I was the new star in *Star Wars* and everything stopped. I was willing myself to breathe. Then J.J. raised a cup of water and said, 'Congratulations.' I was ecstatic. It was probably the happiest day of my life. I've received calls for roles that I'd fought for before, but this felt different. Not only a triumph for me as an actor, but like I was a part of history. That made me really, really happy."

The full cast for *The Force Awakens* was announced about a week after that meeting, with the release of a now-iconic photograph documenting the first read-through of the movie's script. Boyega joined newcomers Daisy Ridley, Oscar Isaac, Adam Driver, and returning cast members Carrie Fisher, Harrison Ford, and Mark Hamill (among others, including R2-D2 in a packing crate). "It was really hard just going through normal life without saying that I'd been cast in *Star Wars*!" said Boyega. "I was really excited when the picture came out with all of us at the read-through. It was historical. It was amazing. I hadn't even told my parents because I was told specifically to keep it quiet. They found out the day of the read-through."

02

03

04

01 Previous page: John Boyega as FN-2187 (AKA. Finn).

02 Boyega and stunt performer Liang Yang rehearsing Finn's lightsaber fight against stormtrooper FN-2199.

03 Boyega with Daisy Ridley, Joonas Suotamo (Chewbacca) and J.J. Abrams on the set of the *Eravana*.

04 Boyega endured the heat of Abu Dhabi in full stormtrooper armor.

05 Finn (Boyega) defended himself against Kylo Ren using Luke Skywalker's lightsaber.

Astonished by the sights that would meet his eyes throughout principal photography, Boyega recalled one particular scene in the Abu Dhabi desert with enthusiasm. "I walked onto that set and saw this huge, life-size TIE fighter, black and red, crushed in the sand. I was literally star-struck," the actor exclaimed. "I was trying to be professional, but every time J.J. came up to me with a note, I was like, 'It's a TIE fighter!'"

The crashed starship offered Boyega some distraction from the reality of wearing full stormtrooper armor in one of the hottest environments on Earth. "I had to wear it in that heat for a couple of days. Let's just say I relied on a combination of sweat, passion, fandom, ice cubes, eye drops, and a lot of water," he noted. "I was drenched in sweat by the time I got out of the stormtrooper outfit. Seeing the TIE fighter next to me made those scenes easier, though."

Thankfully a training regime prior to the start of filming meant Boyega was physically up to the challenge. "For a role like this there's a lot of action, and as actors we needed to learn some hand-to-hand combat and how to use the lightsabers, so I was involved in over seven months of training," explained Boyega, who sometimes worked out to the strains of John Williams' *Star Wars* music playing over speakers at the gym. "I would do some interval training and running, some cardio, skipping, boxing, weight training, all that kind of stuff. When we started filming, I felt like I was really ready."

And just like the Jedi Knights of the saga, the actors got to train with one of the most famous weapons in movie history. "I've always wanted to swing a lightsaber," Boyega admitted. "We were actually working with wooden sticks for a long time to keep safe and get used to the movement [as we] learned the choreography. The lightsabers were really heavy, so you did get a sense of the power that was coming out of this weapon. It really does do something to you, but you do have to be strong, and you have to have skill."

# SLEEPING GIANT

## HOW LUCASFILM STIRRED THE POWER OF THE FORCE

A decade after *Star Wars: Revenge of the Sith* seemingly closed the door on the galactic saga, it fell to a new generation—and some old hands—to bring George Lucas' space fantasy back to theaters.

If *Star Wars* has taught us one thing, it's that there is always hope. Despite *Star Wars: Revenge of the Sith* having completed the narrative circle that began with 1977's *A New Hope*, fans still dreamed that a final trilogy, first hinted at by George Lucas decades before, would eventually grace the silver screen. After the filmmaker sold Lucasfilm to the Walt Disney Company in 2012, it seemed likely that dream was closer to becoming true.

"George Lucas and I sat down when I came to the company, and we started talking about what VII, VIII, and IX might be," recalled Lucasfilm president Kathleen Kennedy, Lucas' hand-picked successor to drive the company he built forward. "Obviously, George had given this a lot of thought beforehand. He had created the first six films, and it's something that had evolved over his entire life. So, he had strong feelings about where those stories would go, and he had created the world in which those stories could be told."

With the saga's creator pursuing new challenges, Kennedy's task was to build a creative team that could continue what Lucas had started.

"Every person who has come to the project has been a huge *Star Wars* fan," Kennedy said of the talent behind the new *Star Wars*. "It's nice to be involved in a movie that everyone cares so much about. And it's not just that they care because they're a fan, but it had something to do with their life. It's something they've drawn from. It's the reason they got into the movie business."

One name familiar to long-term fans of *Star Wars* was Lawrence Kasdan, who joined Michael Arndt and Simon Kinberg on the writing team. Kasdan had penned the screenplays for *Star Wars: The Empire Strikes Back* and *Return of the Jedi*, and Kennedy had been keen to bring him back onboard. "He is one of the icons of the *Star Wars* series," she said. "His sensibility inside these movies is unique. Larry brings to it a sense of humor, but there's an irony in the humor. It's an emotional depth in the humor. He understands characters and understands that banter. He's a real film noir buff and looks back at that fast-talking, 1930s style of dialogue. He infuses that in a very modern way in *Star Wars*."

In addition to writers, the film needed a director capable of realizing a film as energetic and complex as a *Star Wars* picture. "J.J. Abrams was certainly one of my first choices," confirmed Kennedy. "*Star Wars* has this unique sensibility, this combination of adventure and fantasy and humor. There are very few directors who embody all of those sensibilities, and J.J. is one of the few. He was one of the first people I thought of when we were discussing it."

02

03

04

01 Previous page: Daisy Ridley filming a scene as Rey in the Abu Dhabi desert.

02 Writers Lawrence Kasdan (left) and J.J. Abrams (right).

03 Abrams and Oscar Isaac (Poe Dameron) review a shot.

04 Director J.J. Abrams talks Harrison Ford (Han Solo), Joonas Suotamo (Chewbacca), and John Boyega (Finn) through a scene on Starkiller Base.

05 Crewmembers provide shade for John Boyega during filming in Abu Dhabi.

"After I became involved, the question came up as to who was going to direct Episode VII," recalled Kasdan. "Kathy Kennedy was very generous in including me in that process. We went to talk to J.J. Abrams in early 2013 about what he thought a new *Star Wars* would be like. His ideas about what should happen in the next trilogy were like mine, and I was enthusiastic about the idea that he'd direct it. We were all thrilled when he agreed to do it."

For his part, Abrams didn't immediately embrace the opportunity without giving it careful consideration first. "The idea of doing *Star Wars* was terrifying at the beginning. It felt like for every obvious reason, it wasn't the right thing to do," Abrams said of his initial call with Kennedy. "Kathy came in for a meeting, which I expected to be a polite decline, and she started talking about what this movie could be; the creative freedom to do something and the idea of what happens to these characters that we all know and love. She talked about the next step and the new characters that could be the focus of the story. She left the meeting, and I didn't say I didn't want to do it. I told her to let me think about it. My heart was pounding, and my head was racing. I went downstairs to my wife, Katie, and told her I really wanted to do this. We talked about it, and she said that if it was something I really wanted to do, that she understood. She allowed me to imagine what it would be to get involved in *Star Wars*."

Following Arndt's departure from the project in 2013, Abrams and Kasdan set to work on a new script. "One of the most surreal and wonderful things was getting to know and collaborate with Lawrence Kasdan," said Abrams of their partnership. "He's one of the most thoughtful, brilliant, considered, opinionated, funny, collaborative people I've ever met. There I was working on scenes with Han Solo, and Larry would be like, 'I don't think Han would say that. It's not very Han.' I'd be like, okay, and I'd think, 'Well, he would know. He wrote Han Solo in some of the best moments in cinema history.'"

The writers looked back to what had made the original

05

trilogy so memorable—its vibrant and engaging heroes and villains. "The core of this story had to be what makes any story work—the characters," said Abrams. "The fundamental thing that Lawrence Kasdan and I were focusing on, was how to make these characters people that we immediately care about and at least are intrigued by. How do we make them have choices and have behavior that we pull back from, or raise questions about them that we want to understand? It was the thing that was most important for us in the process. We wanted to find characters that we wanted to watch in a story. We knew there would be no shortage of obstacles, and challenges, and evil to throw in their path."

"Right from the start, there was a meeting of minds about the things we wanted the new *Star Wars* to be," Kasdan explained. "How it would be similar to the first trilogy. How would it be different, because times had changed and it's been imitated so much. It's hard to make things look fresh. But all our thoughts were similar. The movies had to get back to tactile [effects and sets], rather than CGI. One of the wonderful things about the first trilogy is that it's kind of funky and puts on a show. There's a tactile feel like we're actually on a set somewhere shooting this movie. All of us wanted to get back to that feeling. So, that was common ground. Then, things that interested us in the story were similar. It was a family saga, and we talked about how we'd continue to play that out in ways that were very interesting not just for new generations but for the people who saw it originally 40 years ago. So, you're paying tribute to a tradition, a saga that has made an impact beyond anyone's imagination. You're trying to be supportive of it, loyal, honest, and respectful of it and at the same time move it forward."

As a sequel to the original trilogy, there was an expectation that characters from those movies would return, but would the likes of Harrison Ford, Carrie Fisher, and Mark Hamill want to? While the movie was still in its very early stages, Lucas and Kennedy made efforts to find out.

“George sat down with Carrie and Mark at *Star Wars* Celebration in Orlando. Harrison was not there, so both George and I went to Harrison after that,” revealed Kennedy. “He told them what the plans were. I think everybody was incredibly excited. There had been talk that there would be more movies. As much as it was a surprise, I don’t think it was a shock. Everybody was keen from the get-go. Everybody was keen to know what we were doing. They wanted to know who was directing and the direction of the story, but they were all excited.”

Kasdan was thrilled to revisit characters he’d last written for in the early 1980s, especially as he would be picking them up in a story set decades later. “It’s great to come back to characters you love. Leia and Han are great people to write for, and now I’ve done it a lot,” he said. “For someone who is their age, there’s a poignancy about how we lose our physical resilience. We deal with many things over a course of a lifetime. Some take a toll and some show up in lines in our face. When you stop resisting it, it can be a glorious thing. You can appreciate and you’re grateful for this journey that put you through so many different paces. When you see Carrie Fisher and you see Harrison Ford, you see all that. We’ve followed them since

06

07

08

they were so young. They grew up on camera. For Harrison, it's been non-stop movie stardom, which is a burden in itself. Very few people have had the long, varied career that Harrison has. He's played fear and aspiration, and had heroism and neuroses. I don't think anyone can watch Harrison walk back onto the *Millennium Falcon* as Han and not be thrilled. He looks so right and so comfortable. In the same way, Carrie Fisher had a cerebral nature at 21 and she's got it now. We're trying to have everyone come through with who they are. The dream in a movie is to bring out what's best in an actor, whether they're 12 or 70. Acting is magical; it's mysterious."

Despite these familiar faces, the focus of the new *Star Wars* would be on a fresh group of younger heroes, led by a desert scavenger named Rey. "We aimed very strongly toward one of the protagonists being a woman right from the get-go," said Kasdan. "There was never a question. It was not just J.J. and I, but Kathy and everyone else involved as well. It cries out for that. Leia was a wonderful character, but she was one of the only women in the original trilogy. This saga demands more in female leadership. We want to see more characters like that. As movies go, we'll see more. We knew that this one had to be centered on both a girl and a boy."

09

06 J.J. Abrams (left) and Lucasfilm President Kathleen Kennedy on the *Millennium Flacon* cockpit set.

07 Carrie Fisher returned to play General Leia Organa in *The Force Awakens*.

08 A traditional chalk clapperboard shows scene V220K was shot on June 26.

09 RAF Greenham Common in Berkshire, England, was the real-world location for the Resistance base on D'Qar.

STAR WARS
EPISODE

11

That boy would be ex-stormtrooper Finn, who would be played by John Boyega. "It was a pitch that Larry Kasdan had when we were talking about the back-story of these characters," explained Abrams. "This idea that there was a guy underneath the uniform that became a main character in the film, and one of our central heroes, was really interesting. The only time we had seen people in stormtrooper uniforms was when Luke and Han put them on to help save Leia. It felt like a great beginning of something. Whether he was a spy, or a turncoat, we knew it was an exciting way into this world. It felt immediately like we hadn't seen it before. It thematically connected to this idea of 'who are these people behind these masks?' All the new characters when we meet them are masked. Kylo-Ren is masked; Rey is masked when you first meet her, and Finn."

Bryan Burk, *The Force Awakens* producer and long-time collaborator with J.J. Abrams, said it was a conscious decision to cast relative unknowns. "Sometimes it feels like you want to bring on new people or find unknown actors so that you can go into the world a little easier and not have to undo what your brain is saying," Burk explained. "In this case, when we started the casting process, we did think that we wanted to find some new actors and some fresh new faces that we could put into the *Star Wars* galaxy. Obviously, it worked spectacularly for George [Lucas] in the original films, so we decided to continue that." Daisy Ridley was the fortunate actor who secured the role of Rey, the new saga's central protagonist. "We looked for a long time at many people. What we were looking for was someone who felt that she was capable of everything," said Abrams. "It's a crazy thing, but this character needed to be brought to life by an actor that didn't have limitations. We needed someone who was going to be vulnerable, tough, terrified, thoughtful, sweet, and confused to take on the burden of this role and do it with authenticity.

"We needed someone who is able to go to this deeply emotional state and do it again and again, in some cases with brand-new actors; in other cases, with actors that didn't exist at all, and in other cases, legendary

10 Previous page: The cast and crew of *Star Wars: The Force Awakens* gathered at Pinewood Studios.

11 J.J. Abrams framing a shot on the Niima Outpost set in Abu Dhabi.

12 John Boyega and Daisy Ridley pose in costume on the *Millennium Falcon* set.

13 Ridley (Rey) with director Abrams during the Abu Dhabi shoot.

12

13

actors," the director continued. "She needed to do all of this, and on top of everything, be an unknown. I didn't want someone who everyone knew who you had seen before. We found some great people, but it wasn't until we found Daisy that we thought we'd found the person who can do that sweet, light stuff; she has an incredible smile. She's beautiful. She could do the spirited stuff as well as the tough and emotional."

"*Star Wars* delivers on different levels," said Kathleen Kennedy of breathing new life into the saga. "I think all of us were quite amazed when we started to pick it apart and discovered what incredibly good storytelling it was. How simple it was and how spare it was. And how much fun! It made us appreciate what we all have to do. It had already been done so well, that our job was to interpret what had been done so well and make it our own. We needed to understand what was working about it and why it resonated with so many people on so many levels. When you do a movie like this, you have to take it seriously. You can't treat it like lightweight storytelling. Everything George did was serious. It drew upon tried and true mythology, a basis of all religious thought, family values, and key values around aspiration. What does it mean to make people feel like they can do anything? If they live their life well, they can achieve greatness. Those are the values inherent in *Star Wars*. You don't want to make that pedantic and pretentious, so you need to find a way to preserve those values and make it fun and have it be an adventure, and carry through with that. That's what we spent our focus on—isolating all these elements inside the *Star Wars* mythology and doing the best job we could to emulate what George created."

# SCOUNDREL'S LUCK

## HARRISON FORD: HAN SOLO

Han Solo was a man who'd spent his early years running away from responsibility, but that all changed when he met Luke Skywalker and threw his lot in with Princess Leia Organa and the Rebel Alliance. However, after his son, Ben, turned to the dark side of the Force and his relationship with Leia suffered as a result, Solo ran back to his former life as a smuggler rather than confront the trauma of such losses.

Screen legend Harrison Ford didn't take much persuading to reprise the role that had made his name. "I had a degree of self-interest," he told *Star Wars Insider* about playing Han Solo again. "I was very gratified when I first saw the script and thought there were some amazing ideas; interesting things to do. Then I was very excited for the opportunity to work with J.J. Abrams, whom I've known for a long time."

J.J. Abrams had written 1991's *Regarding Henry*, in which Ford had starred. Another attraction for the actor was the opportunity to work with Kathleen Kennedy again, whom he'd known since the making of the original *Indiana Jones* trilogy in the 1980s. "Of course, people are a very important part of the mix," Ford said. "I have a very long and fruitful relationship with Kathy Kennedy, so I was glad to be able to work with her again. I thought it was going to be fun. I knew that the film would be in good hands, but that wasn't the only attraction to the project for me."

In *The Force Awakens*, audiences would meet a Han Solo who had been rocked by the punches life had thrown at him, and Ford was interested to learn what writer and director Abrams had mapped out for the character. "We had discussions about development of Han and his relationship to other characters in the story," confirmed Ford. "They were very interesting and encouraging conversations. Then there was some work done in respect of the questions I had, or input that I had with J.J., and I was pleased with that. But I'm a 'get on at the beginning and off at the end' kind of guy, so I don't really remember the street signs along the way."

On set, the actor's excitement about working with Abrams was justified. "[J.J.] is an enormously skilled filmmaker and a very efficient director and producer. He brought a real sincerity and emotional understanding, which was something I was very pleased to see," said Ford. "He's very thoughtful and very wise about human nature and the development of character and relationships. It was a real pleasure to work with him and all of the members of his team as the film went on."

Having worked with many directors over the decades, including George Lucas, Irvin Kershner, and Richard Marquand on the original *Star Wars* trilogy, Ford admitted that the level of input he'd had on the characters he'd played differed from movie to movie.

"Over the course of making the *Star Wars* films, we worked with three different directors, and each of them had a different style and attitude towards the process," the actor confirmed. "I would say that the relationship with those three directors was different, but I always felt that there was a degree of collaboration that was comfortable for everybody involved."

Set several decades after the original trilogy's climax in *Star Wars: Return of the Jedi*, the First Order era took many familiar designs, including the iconic stormtrooper armor, and updated them, while other elements such as Han Solo's battered space freighter, the *Millennium Falcon*, were painstakingly recreated. Just as Solo announced in *The Force Awakens* trailer, standing on the ship's set was like coming home for Ford.

02

03

01 Previous page: Harrison Ford as Han Solo.

02 Ford on location during exterior filming of scenes on Takodana.

03 Harrison Ford (right) with J.J. Abrams (center) and Joonas Suotamo (Chewbacca) on the *Eravana* set.

04 Han Solo and Chewbacca reunited.

04

"I spent a lot of years there, so it was fun to see it again," he said. "I didn't remember it as well as I thought I did. There are things I remember about the cockpit and the funny stuff we went through. On the original cockpit, I asked George to let us get into it, so we could try it on for size. Finally, we did get a chance, Chewbacca [Peter Mayhew] and I, to walk into the cockpit. Of course, he couldn't get into the seat! Flying it developed a little bit between iterations of the first three films, but it started to come back to me. It was fun."

In the movie, Solo becomes something of a mentor to new heroes Rey and Finn. How did Ford find his young co-stars, Daisy Ridley and John Boyega? "They are both very engaging personalities; both in their real lives and in their screen characters," he said. "I think the audiences will be delighted to make their acquaintance and follow them through the story. They're both very inventive and spirited presences. Their characters are very interesting and go through some changes. The casting has been brilliant, in both cases."

Ford was convinced that *The Force Awakens* would appeal to a new generation of fans by harking back to themes that were present in the original movies. "The genius of *Star Wars* has always been this science fiction, fantasy context, but underpinned by an emotionally recognizable human story that we all relate to, by degree," suggested the actor. "We all recognize the power of these relationships, and the complications in people's lives, and it's made these films so important to pass on from generation to generation. You can call them family films, but they are iconic representations of what we know about the complications of our lives."

# ALWAYS ROYALTY

## CARRIE FISHER: LEIA ORGANA

Former senator and a veteran of the Galactic Civil War, General Leia Organa recognized the imminent threat posed by the First Order and organized the Resistance to defend the values of the New Republic.

Carrie Fisher's performance as Princess Leia in the original trilogy redefined our idea of what a princess in peril would look like. Feisty, witty, tough, and very much in control, Leia led the charge, both into battle and in propelling iconic feminist roles into the mainstream of popular culture.

"I have people come up to me and say that my character inspired them to live their lives the way they did," said Fisher of the groundbreaking rebel leader created by George Lucas for *A New Hope*. "There was a playful side that people got out of it, and there was the side of it where you thought of yourself as being capable. The princess is someone who takes responsibility for her life and makes choices and has a life. She doesn't fall into things."

The Leia of *The Force Awakens* is recognizably the same person, with the same values and determination. "I am Princess Leia. Princess Leia is me. It's like a Mobius strip. My life has informed who she is, and she's informed who I am and who I've had to be, based on the experiences I've gone through and the courage that was required to go through some of that. So, a lot of her demeanor, her passion and her willingness to go on, I've found in me. Nothing has changed, except the hair," Fisher joked. "I wanted to use the iconic hairstyle that I had initially. I wanted that hairstyle back. If nothing else, I wanted little old Leia to walk by a window wearing that hairdo on the way to the bathtub. Just show it once. But no, I guess they thought it would be too distracting."

Recognizing the cultural importance of the original trilogy, Fisher said of her many fans, "This is their fairytale. This is what they grew up with, what their fantasies were propelled by. It was this other world. They belong to that other world, and they feel a part of that. They feel like they know you and to an extent they do. The funniest thing to me, and the sweetest thing to me, is when they bring you a three-week-old child wearing the Leia outfit. It's also seeing these tiny kids, and the children know who you are. That's the oddest, sweetest, most fascinating aspect of it."

And how did she feel those fans would react to the new chapter in the space fantasy saga? "I think the fans will be happy to be in their home away from home again," Fisher answered.

Fisher was also keen to point out that director J.J. Abrams was a fan himself. "What I felt like with J.J. is that he loved these films," she said. "It's not part of your history; it's part of your childhood. Little kids grew up watching this, and J.J. is one of those. And there's a tremendous responsibility to this thing that he treasured. He was taking that seriously. He was excited by it. There's responsibility that goes with that, and he seemed completely up for that. J.J. is someone who's proven he can do these epic, otherworldly films, and also worldly films. He's a writer and a director and he loves movies. That really comes across."

With a few decades having passed between the making of *A New Hope* and Episode VII, *Insider* asked Fisher whether the experiences felt any different. "We've moved on," she said. "I have more experience to bring to what I'm looking at; to bring to bear upon the situation. I was an innocent; I was moving faster when I was a kid when we were making those films. So, now I'm looking at it with a lot more experience."

The author and actor was enthused by the qualities of the new members of the *Star Wars* family joining the cast for *The Force Awakens*. "I was nervous and excited," she said. "We had a good time together. Everyone was nervous in different ways. Watching Daisy Ridley, she grew enormously through the process of filming. She's very confident, very at ease. So, it's definitely a home to her. John Boyega always seemed comfortable. He came into the situation very confident, ready to get at it."

She had high praise for Adam Driver's commitment to playing the film's bad guy, Kylo Ren. "Playing a villain, you don't know you're a villain. This is your cause, and this is what Adam is doing. He's passionate, but he's also solitary," she said. Fisher was also thrilled to be working with some of her original co-stars again, including Anthony Daniels as C-3PO. "He looks exactly the same! It's a school reunion. It's a *Star Wars* high school reunion."

02

03

01 Previous page: Carrie Fisher as General Leia Organa.

02 Fisher and Daisy Ridley filming Leia and Rey's farewell on location at RAF Greenham Common.

03 Fisher's daughter Billie Lourd played Lieutenant Connix in the movie.

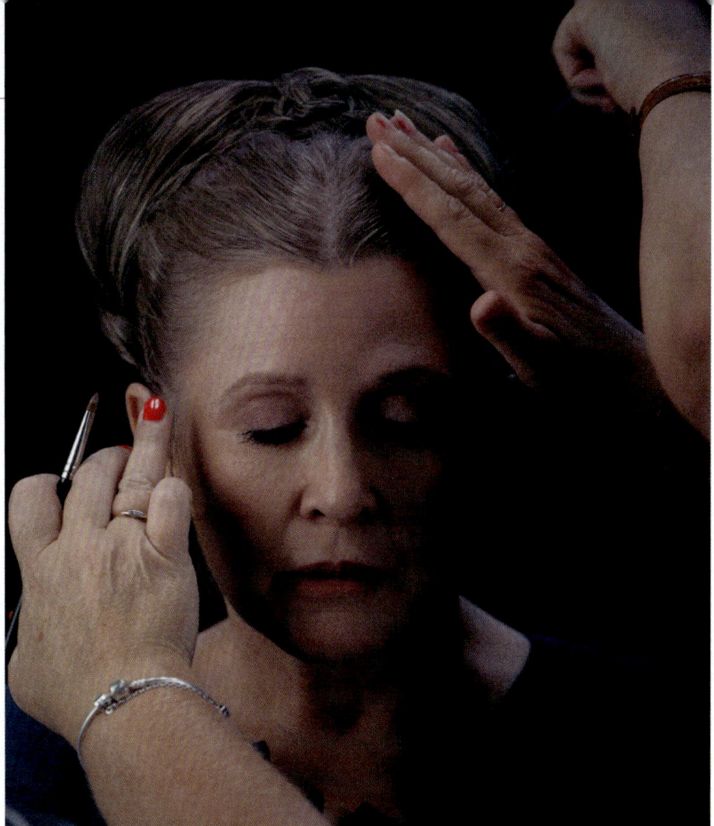

04

05

06

04 Fisher had hoped Leia's original bun hairstyle would feature in the movie.

05 General Leia Organa and Nien Nunb help plan the attack on Starkiller Base.

06 Director J.J. Abrams on set with Carrie Fisher as Leia.

# BEING BB-8

**BB-8 became a global megastar the instant the spherical droid rolled across the screen in the trailer for *Star Wars: The Force Awakens*. Puppeteers Brian Herring and Dave Chapman reveal how they gave a metal ball such a vibrant personality.**

"I saw *Star Wars: A New Hope* in the December it came out in the U.K. My dad took my brother and I to the Harlow Odeon to see it, and it blew my mind. I was obsessed with the film until well into my teens," remembers Brian Herring, one of the two lead puppeteers behind BB-8. "Rather than go to university when I was 18, I looked for work as an actor instead," he continued. "My first job was in a touring pantomime, and when I wasn't acting, I'd do stage managing or a bit of stand-up comedy. I wound up having an audition for a satirical TV series called *Spitting Image* (1984-1996). They taught me how to operate the puppets, and six weeks later I was on television. They had me in for a couple of days a week as a trainee puppeteer back in 1992, learning under some of the best puppeteers in Britain at the time, and I've been a professional puppeteer ever since."

Dave Chapman saw *Star Wars* at the cinema when he was five years old, "The same year I first saw the Muppets, and knew what I wanted to do as a job when I was older," he told *Insider*. "I figured out how Muppet characters were made, and I even made a few puppets myself, but I quickly realized I was more of a performer than a maker. From the age of 11 I was writing to people saying, 'I want to do this. Can you give me some advice?' I even wrote to Jim Henson saying I wanted work at the company, and although they wrote back to say I was too young, they promised to keep my details on file.

"I knew I couldn't walk into that kind of job from school, so I went through drama college as a stage manager and worked in theater in London's West End after I graduated," Chapman continued. "Then, half a lifetime later, my mom left a message on my answering machine telling me the Jim Henson Company were auditioning for people to train to be Muppet performers. It turned out they really had kept my letter on file. I went to the audition and was chosen to be trained to work at Henson doing Muppets and puppets and monsters and creatures. That was my green-for-go into the business."

Both puppeteers were understandably excited to learn that a new *Star Wars* feature film was being made, and it would be shot in the U.K.

Herring recalled, "I was chatting about the industry to Neal Scanlan (*The Force Awakens* creature and special make-up effects creative supervisor), and I said to him, 'I need to find out who's doing the creatures for *Star Wars* and kick their door in,' and Neal said, 'Don't do that, I like the door where it is!' Neal hired me to be puppetry consultant for *The Force Awakens*, and I was there for 16 months, right through to the end of principal photography.

01

"I was initially working with Paul Casey on the luggabeast and the happabore, and then we started getting designs for this little thing called 'snow globe,' which eventually became BB-8. Josh Lee made a little puppet of the droid, and I started to work with it to show J.J. Abrams (the director) what we could achieve with half a ball on a ball. We shot some test footage, and then the rest of the team got involved. Matt Denton started building things and programming them, Giles Hannigan and Jake Lunt Davies were designing, and then Neal said, 'I'm assuming you want Dave to work on this?' and I said, 'Oh yeah!' Dave had been working with us on some research and development for other stuff, but after that it was Dave and me. We started our rehearsals, and the rest is history."

Imbuing the illusion of a personality into a prop that looked like a robotic beachball involved a lot of development work.

"We did a great deal of preparation," explained Chapman. "Everything you saw on screen was worked out long before it went before the camera. We shot stuff, tried different things, and camera tested everything, so by the time we got to shooting we knew it very well."

"When we did our tests, we'd go away for a couple of days with a video camera and film a few bits and pieces, then Neal Scanlan would come and look at them, and tell us what he'd liked," Herring added.

"When working in tandem with someone, you work so closely together that you don't need to talk," Chapman said. "Whether I was working with Matt Denton or Brian, we all knew what that movement vocabulary was and what BB-8 would do in any given circumstance."

The process was akin to learning a dance routine.

"We looked at the scripts and thought about where a scene would go, so we were always meticulously rehearsed," said Chapman. "There's definitely a flexibility and freedom within that, which I think is really healthy. Sometimes J.J. Abrams would suggest trying something different. Sometimes we'd riff a bit and run with it, but most things we wanted we looked at beforehand because it's cheaper to rehearse in a workshop than it is to rehearse on set."

"And we rehearsed with the BB-8 you see on screen. It would have been too expensive otherwise," Herring revealed.

01 Previous page: Brian Herring with BB-8 during filming of *Star Wars: The Last Jedi*.

02 BB-8 concept art by Jake Lunt Davies.

03 One early concept for BB-8 featured tire treads across the droid's spherical body. Concept art by Christian Alzmann.

04

04 Brian Herring propels BB-8 across the Abu Dhabi sands.

05 "In my head, he was Poe Dameron's dog," said Herring.

06 The prop used for close-up shots of BB-8 was known as "the wiggler."

07 Dave Chapman during production of *The Last Jedi*.

That didn't mean that there weren't several BB-8s available to the puppeteers, each with its own unique adaptation.

"There were seven different versions of BB-8 on *The Force Awakens*, each of which was operated in a different way," said Chapman. "There was the puppet version, which was the one used the most on *The Force Awakens*. It had rods at the back, which gave me control of the body and the pitch, and roll control on the head so I could make it go left, right, forwards, and backwards on the body. I positioned the head while Dave controlled the eyeline, which was technically very difficult because he was watching via a monitor. Between us we had to make everything work.

"There were two trike versions, which had an axel that BB-8 spun on via a drive unit on the back. Whenever the trikes come out, Matt Denton drove. Dave had complete control of the head on that one, and I was off somewhere flashing lights and beeping. There was a bowling ball version; there was a "bomb-drop" version with a mechanism in the head, which was the one audiences saw going up and down in the X-wings. And there was a carrying version, which was seen when Finn (John Boyega) loaded BB-8 into the hatch on the *Falcon*.

"Then there was a close-up version called the wiggler, which was fixed on a plate. We could either bury the plate in sand or fix it to the floor of, say, the *Millennium Falcon*. That had 359 degrees of movement on the body and the head. I controlled the body and head while Dave ran the lights. ILM worked on practically every BB-8 shot apart from the wiggler, which was untouched."

Beyond the physical challenges of operating BB-8, the puppeteers combined their acting talent and imagination when aiming to convey the droid's personality.

"You always have to find the character," asserted Chapman. "You have to do that no matter how the technology is being utilized. We decided early on BB-8 was like a kid brother, or a small dog who wanted to be Rey's friend."

05

06

"In my head, he was Poe Dameron's dog," said Herring. "You apply that to the story; Poe sends his dog away on a mission, Rey finds a stray dog, and looks after it until she gets it home. When we were shooting the scene when Rey first finds BB-8 and he has the bent antenna, she just takes it out of his head and BB-8 looks back up at her. When she goes to put it back into place, he puts his head back down again. We did it again in *The Last Jedi*, when she finally gets on the *Falcon*, and then at the end of *The Rise of Skywalker* when Rey gets out of the X-wing and BB-8 goes over to her, she does it again. I remember saying to Daisy, 'Shall we do the aerial thing again?' and she thought it would be lovely. It's their little bonding moment. You don't program robots to do that. Very, very early on in the original trilogy C-3PO does a double take. You don't program a droid to do a double take."

Chapman and Herring faced several memorable challenges with BB-8 during the making of *The Force Awakens.*

07

08

08 BB-8's "thumbs up" was one of Herring's favorite shots to film.

09 Rey fixing BB-8's antenna became a recurring theme throughout the sequel trilogy.

"One thing we didn't think we'd ever be able to do were the stairs in Maz Kanata's castle," recalled Herring. "We tried it on normal stairs, but his body was too big, it wouldn't stop, it wouldn't rest. We did a set walk through and I said to our second assistant director, Joey Coughlin, 'Do we really need to do these stairs?' and he said no. That was on a Monday. When we got onto the set on Wednesday, Joey said, 'J.J. wants you to come down a couple of these stairs,' so we had to quickly work it out. BB-8 doesn't like stairs so, if you look, what we did was I pushed the head forward and Dave had BB-8 give a little look left and right and check every single step as he goes down. Originally it was supposed to be just two or three of the stairs, but then J.J. said, 'Can you go back a bit further?' People assumed that when they saw BB-8 coming down those stairs it was done digitally. But no, it was all practical."

Chapman noted the very first shot of BB-8 ever revealed. "He was 'running' through the desert, which was Brian pushing him at very high speeds, while I was strapped to the back of the camera car, looking at a monitor and operating the head. I said to J.J. afterwards, 'I kind of looked down the lens. Do you want to do another one, because it kind of looks like I looked at the audience?' And he was like, 'No, it's fine, it's like he's saying, 'Hey, look at me, I'm so fast!" To my great surprise it turned out to be the first shot of BB-8 from the movie anyone got to see!"

"The thumbs-up scene with Finn was a definite, definite high point for me, because that was all done with the puppet," Herring added. "We shot it quite quickly. As he's looking backwards and forwards, left and right, Dave hit his eyelines brilliantly and it just worked. We had to make sure his body was in the right place because ILM were going to replace that panel and have a little blow torch pop out. When a scene like that comes off right, and then when it gets such a laugh in the film, it's lovely."

# HOT SHOT

## OSCAR ISAAC: POE DAMERON

In search of information as to the whereabouts of Luke Skywalker, ace Resistance starfighter pilot Poe Dameron bore witness to the vile cruelty of the First Order on Jakku. Tortured by Kylo Ren then rescued by a rogue stormtrooper he renamed Finn, Dameron went on to lead the Resistance attack on Starkiller Base.

orn in Guatemala in 1979, Oscar Isaac has never known a world without *Star Wars*. "It was a big part of my family. My uncle, cousin, and brother were huge fans, and they collected all the toys, so by proxy, I was also a fan," Poe Dameron actor Oscar Isaac explained to *Insider*. "The first film I remember seeing as a child was *Star Wars: Return of the Jedi*. I think for a lot of people in the film business in general, *Star Wars* is a milestone. For some people, it's why they do what they do, so to be asked to be a part of it was a huge, huge honor, and it just created such excitement."

Isaac recalled how director J.J. Abrams initially outlined his vision for the new film to him during their early meetings. "J.J. spoke about how he wanted to approach the film by going back to the roots of [*Star Wars*] and shooting on film, making it a very textured world," said Isaac. "As far as the performances, it felt like he saw things on three levels. One was visually the story that was being told, so you could turn it to silent and still have communicated what was happening emotionally. Secondly, it was the energy, which is really the thrust of the whole thing—the proper level of energy for any given scene. Then third was the nuance of the characters and how they would interact with each other, what they would say, how they'd respond, and how that would reveal who the characters were.

"So, that was interesting to play with and make suggestions [as to] how those three things were affected and how they could be highlighted," Isaac continued. "That was the fascinating thing about playing Poe; It is a specific color that he adds to the film. It's one that's energetic. There's almost an old-school, Cary Grant in *His Girl Friday* (1994) kind of speed to it, and that's something that J.J. really liked."

As a lifelong fan of the *Star Wars* movies, Isaac cited the saga's human element as being an important part of their appeal. "In the original films, I think that's what was so moving about them," he said. "I remember when I saw *Return of the Jedi*, what stuck in my head was that moment when Darth Vader took his helmet off and Luke Skywalker saw his father as this vulnerable being. He was not this huge, black monolith; He was suddenly this vulnerable man, and that's a big moment in a child's life when you realize your parents are not immortal gods. Those are universal themes, along with the quest for identity, the feeling that you're lost and you don't know where you fit in."

Something Isaac really appreciated about the project was the inclusive atmosphere on set that made him feel welcome in the *Star Wars* galaxy. "I think that's because of J.J. Abrams, who allowed people to feel ownership over it," the actor asserted. "You're not just being allowed to come into this world, this is *your* world, and you get to add to it. You get to really live out these characters and be part of this world."

01 Previous page: Oscar Isaac as Poe Dameron.

02 *The Force Awakens* begins with Dameron's mission to Jakku in search of Luke Skywalker.

03 J.J. Abrams and Oscar Isaac during the filming of Finn and Poe Dameron's escape from the First Order.

04 Shooting the TIE fighter escape sequence interiors.

05 Isaac (right) rehearsing a scene with John Boyega (center) and J.J. Abrams on the Resistance base set.

02

03

Not only that, but Isaac got to work alongside actors (and characters) he'd idolized since childhood. "That was when it really felt surreal; when you'd see Carrie Fisher and Harrison Ford, C-3PO and R2-D2, and Chewbacca. Those are icons in the flesh. That's when you got a little bit of chills like, 'Wow, this is actually happening!'" Isaac said. "They were great, particularly Carrie, who was so funny. I found her to be very kind and it was a lot of fun to shoot with her. She still remembered all the lines from the old films, so she'd just launch into the opening of *A New Hope* where Leia leaves the message in R2-D2. It was pretty incredible."

Isaac also had kind words for his co-star John Boyega. "John is a fantastic human being. I really, really have a lot of affection for him," the actor said. "He reminds me a lot of my little brother, actually. He's incredibly flexible and on his toes, with different ideas. He

04

05

had a huge responsibility, and I think that he [carried] it with a lot of grace and generosity."

Isaac attributed that same sensibility to everyone involved with bringing *Star Wars* back to the big screen. "What's great is that this has been done with no cynicism and with such love and enthusiasm from everybody, starting with J.J.," he said. "I think that's going to be infectious. You'll be able to feel that coming off the screen; just the love of *Star Wars* and the love of these stories and being able to add new ones to the legacy. Obviously, they mean so much to everyone. That's a difficult and scary thing, because everyone has a very specific idea of what [*Star Wars*] should be. But I think when you approach it with this much love and generosity, that stuff becomes less important. You see that J.J. is someone who loves it so much and has found people that love it just as much, and who want to make it special and beautiful."

# FALLEN SON

## ADAM DRIVER: KYLO REN

A servant of the dark side of the Force, Kylo Ren was originally Ben Solo, the son of Han Solo and Leia Organa. Manipulated and cajoled by Snoke, Supreme Leader of the First Order, from a young age, the boy could never escape the shadow cast by his late grandfather, Darth Vader.

"I think it was the last day of shooting *Girls* and I got a phone call to see if I was interested in meeting J.J. Abrams to talk about *Star Wars*," said Adam Driver, who played the movie's dark villain, Kylo Ren. "I thought that it would be interesting to do, so I said 'yes.' A month later, I left for Los Angeles, and I met J.J. to talk about the role. Then I met with Lucasfilm president Kathleen Kennedy, who talked more about it. I was very excited; It was such a big thing and I'd never done anything quite like it."

However, the prospect of playing a character whose face, for much of his screen time, would be hidden beneath a mask gave Driver pause for thought. "Wearing a mask is quite a challenging thing," he admitted to *Insider*, adding that the prospect "was very scary and terrifying, so it wasn't immediately a 'yes.' Actually, I thought about it quite a bit, even though it was kind of a no-brainer, but I didn't want to take it lightly."

Ultimately the actor was convinced by director Abrams, who walked Driver through everything he wanted the movie to be. "He talked about how he wanted to start it and the themes that he was going with. He talked about things that inspired him that he and Lawrence Kasdan were already working on," Driver recalled. "J.J. had ideas that were very clear in his mind about the conventions that he wanted to upturn and things that grounded Kylo Ren as a character. Character was something that he talked about the most. I feel like some movies are so heavy on special effects or visuals that a lot of things get lost as far as two people talking to one another. And that was something that J.J. stressed from the beginning; It was all character—there was hardly any talk of special effects. It was all about grounding these people in a reality, even though it's a long time ago in a galaxy far away. If no one cares about what's happening, or no one believes that these are people are real, then you won't care about any of it."

An important element of the role, and one that would help Driver shape his performance, was the inherent challenge of Kylo Ren's costume, designed by Michael Kaplan. "I'd go in for three or four days and put all this stuff on, the mask and the costume, shoot, then put it away for a few weeks," said Driver of the fittings and screen tests leading up to principal photography. "I'd fly in to see what they were coming up with. There were nods to Akira Kurosawa and all those samurai references, like the way his jacket bows out just a little bit. My only input was whether it felt good or bad. I was involved in making it functional, which

02

03

04

01 Previous page: Adam Driver as Kylo Ren.

02 Kylo Ren removed his helmet only twice in *The Force Awakens*: while interrogating Rey, and later when meeting his father, Han Solo, on Starkiller Base.

03 In preparation for the role of Kylo Ren, Driver spent four hours per day lightsaber training.

04 Adam Driver during a costume fitting with designer Michael Kaplan.

05 Filming Kylo Ren's duel with Rey at Pinewood Studios, England.

was great. They were all about how they could make it more efficient and something that someone could wear. It looks great, but if you can't move in it or breathe in it, then it doesn't make sense for the audience or the actor."

During filming, Driver began to find the costume freeing. "There are so many layers to Kylo Ren anyway, it was interesting to find out who he was with the mask on or with the mask off, and that was part of our initial conversations. There's something empowering for someone to completely hide themselves in a mask that is so intimidating."

Channeling the physicality of the character was less of a challenge for the actor, who had previously served as a U.S. Marine before becoming an actor.

"One of the first things that I wanted to do, as soon as everything was all scheduled, was to start drilling daily and making it part of my daily life," said Driver. "I had three months to prepare, so I wanted to immerse myself in the training as much as possible. The first week was four hours a day of fight training; just stretching and going over the training with sticks and gradually building up to the lightsaber. Then I went to New York and worked with people they sent there. Whenever we weren't on set, I was always with the fight guys. It was almost like a play in a way, the dancing part of fighting. There was a structure, and it was important to know where everything was going. You always learn new things about it, and for me it was a process whereby a lot of the external things had been formed that gave me more information. Usually, I feel like I try to work internally and try to think about how it feels from the inside out, but for this there were so many tactile things that I could actually hold on to that gave me a lot of information. The fight choreography was one of them."

For all the special effects, exotic creatures, and action sequences, as far as Driver is concerned it is the grounded nature of *Star Wars* that is the saga's biggest attraction, as both an actor and a fan.

"I think the great thing about *Star Wars* is that, yes, it's a long time ago in a galaxy far, far away, and there are spaceships and lightsabers, but the family story and the friendship and sacrifice elements are really big, human themes that make it enduring," he suggested. "All those human things are what connected people to the movies in the first place."

# REAL TO REEL

## THE BACK-TO-BASICS APPROACH OF MAKING *STAR WARS: THE FORCE AWAKENS*

From the outset, Lucasfilm endeavored to lend the new *Star Wars* movie a tangible, physical quality using practical props, effects, and concepts that paid homage to the visual style of the original trilogy.

yself and J.J. [Abrams] talked right away about real creatures and real sets," said Kathleen Kennedy about recreating the feel of the early *Star Wars* films. "It's a grounded sensibility that goes back to the first three movies. I've always had a feeling inside the world of special effects where it's so important to give the audience what's familiar, in a grounded way, even though the stories take place in outer space. That was important to J.J., too. What he loved more than anything were the tactile sensibilities inside the first three movies. All of the design began with that premise. We sat down and immediately talked about what we could build for real, where could we shoot real locations, and how much of the movie we could design in that way."

That process began with months of detailed research and conceptualizing, generating ideas before a shooting script was even completed. "Research was an interesting process for this film," explained producer Bryan Burk. "Visiting George Lucas' archives was unlike anything I've ever seen before. It was literally a journey through my entire childhood. To have had the opportunity to see all this amazing artwork done by all of these wonderful artists was incredible. There were so many things to look at in every corner and at every turn; it was a bombardment of inspiration.

"And because it's *Star Wars,* there are numerous people out in the world who are die-hard fans, a lot of whom happen to be our friends," Burk continued. "Meeting people like Pablo Hidalgo at Lucasfilm, who are beyond experts on the world of *Star Wars* and know everything about it, was an invaluable aid in making this film."

The team that Lucasfilm brought together to bring their vision to reality included some of cinema's most creative talents, as Burk outlined. "Rick Carter, the production designer, had worked with Kathleen Kennedy for years on numerous movies. He's a genius, like no production designer I'd ever worked with, in the sense that for him it wasn't just about the look of the movie, it was about the feel of the movie, and the tone of the movie. We talked about the story with Rick, who was involved in all the story meetings throughout the entire process. He understood the franchise and the film itself—what we wanted it to be, and what Kathy wanted it to be."

Costume designer Michael Kaplan had collaborated with J.J. Abrams on *Mission: Impossible III* (2006) and both of the director's *Star Trek* films. "We've been fans of Michael's forever," said Burk. "He began his career with *Blade Runner* and eight gazillion movies since then. So, the opportunity to work with him yet again, let alone on something as iconic and personal for all of us, was undeniable."

01

02

03

04

01 Entrance gate to Niima Outpost. Concept art by Matt Allsopp.

02 The on-location set based on Allsopp's concept.

03 The Abu Dhabi set for the Niima Outpost depot.

04 Concept art of the depot by Erik Tiemens.

01

Dan Mindel was another alumni from Abram's *Mission Impossible* crew and was director of photography. "Not only does Dan have such a beautiful eye when he's looking at things, but his entire team is a pleasure to work with," Burk declared. "They are constantly bringing new ideas to the table, finding new ways to shoot things and constantly inventing things that we've never seen before on film."

Special makeup effects artist Neal Scanlan came out of semi-retirement to run the movie's creature shop, following in the footsteps of the original trilogy's Stuart Freeborn. "There are not a lot of people who are making puppets today, let alone creatures, and let alone tangible ones," Burk said of Scanlan's pedigree. "It's a craft that I'd never seen first-hand until I had the opportunity to work with Neal and his team. I'm hoping that many other films will start embracing the long-lost craft of creating creatures and tangible co-stars."

"The work that Neal Scanlan and his team have done, and the artists we've been able to bring into the process, just pushed it and pushed it," agreed Kennedy. "The technology inside that tactile world has improved to the same extent that the CG world has improved. It's been very rewarding to see what people can bring in front of the camera and to be able to look at dailies. It seems like such a new and modern conceit to be sitting in dailies and looking at real things, instead of blue screen waiting for things to come months later. For the cast to be able to act in an environment where they've got real creatures and sets that they can touch and interact with makes a difference. It immediately feels real."

06

05

07

05 First Order stormtrooper concept art by Glyn Dillon.

06 TIE fighter crash site concept art by Andrée Wallin.

07 The sleek stormtroopers of *The Force Awakens*.

08

## What a Piece of Junk!

According to Lydia Fry, the film's assistant art director, one of the difficulties regarding the *Millennium Falcon* set was that there were no plans of the inside of the ship, so they had to rely on deleted footage and set stills.

"There were lots of little quirks within the *Millennium Falcon*," Fry explained. "For example, there are certain areas of the ship, like the doorway going into the cockpit, that were only ever shown from the inside of the cockpit, never from the corridor. A deleted scene from *The Empire Strikes Back* showed it was relatively plain, but because it had only been seen in a deleted scene on a DVD, we were able to add our own detail to it."

09

10

11

12

08 The *Millennium Falcon* revealed. Concept art by Andrée Wallin.

09 The main corridor of the *Millennium Falcon* set.

10 The *Falcon* hold set was a painstaking recreation of the original from *A New Hope*.

11 The chase on Jakku. Concept art by Doug Chiang.

12 Han Solo and Chewie arrive on the *Falcon*. Concept art by Matt Allsopp.

13

## Maz Kanata's Castle

"The castle was the center of not only the film, but the center of the story," explained set decorator Lee Sandales. "A lot of things were revealed there. Everything about *The Force Awakens* happened at Maz's castle. It was the one set that took me a long time to get into my head. First of all, the concept of a *Star Wars* castle. It was really difficult to actually achieve that because it wasn't just a castle—it was a place where every kind of being from the galaxy would come to. It was kind of a home for pirates. Some of them were pretty shady characters. I had a lot of fun with it. The inspiration came from a Ralph McQuarrie drawing of a single lamp. And, from there, I was able to develop the whole world of all the dressings, all the fixtures, all the fittings, all the furniture, all the fabrics."

14

15

16

13 The entrance to Maz Kanata's castle. Concept art by Thom Tenery.

14 Background artists in creature costumes take instruction from director J.J. Abrams on the castle interior set.

15 Han Solo, Rey, and BB-8 inside Maz's castle. Concept art by Matt Allsopp.

16 Maz Kanata concept art by Glyn Dillon.

## Starkiller Base

According to co-production designer Darren Gilford, the design of the entire planet that housed the First Order's superweapon was inspired by a prop from *A New Hope.* "One of J.J. Abrams' favorite references was Luke's Jedi training ball, the one he used aboard the *Millennium Falcon* when he first trained with Obi-Wan Kenobi," said Gilford. "So, we studied that ball, its graphic nature, the repetitive details, and so on. Then we said, 'What if that was a planet?' That was where we started in imagining what Starkiller Base would look like."

17

17 General Hux's address to First Order troops on Starkiller Base. Concept art by James Clyne.

18 Early concept art by James Clyne for Starkiller Base, which took inspiration from the training remote from *A New Hope.*

19 The forest where Rey and Kylo Ren fought was built on a sound stage at Pinewood Studios.

# PURE GOLD

## ANTHONY DANIELS: C-3PO

For a humble protocol droid, built from spare parts by Anakin Skywalker, C-3PO had experienced more than most dedicated adventurers by the time the Galactic Civil War ended. But his travails were far from over as the First Order flexed its might and made plans to dominate the galaxy.

t's odd for me to realize that 40 years of my life have been spent playing C-3PO," said Anthony Daniels when *Insider* asked the actor about playing the character again in *The Force Awakens.* "I'm the only person to be involved in all seven movies, which is really strange. One of the reasons that it is possible is because C-3PO isn't human. He's very human inside: He gets old inside, and he gets more tired and cranky inside, but on the outside he's just who you first met back in 1977. For a lot of people, that's a very strong connection."

Part of that connection comes from the protocol droid's permanently friendly expression, Daniels suggested. "From the concept art, they created a face that has spoken to millions of people around the world. It has connected with them and given them memories for three generations now. When I look at him, I still have that feeling. C-3PO's face gives the impression that he's thinking and that he cares; That he's afraid. He's always afraid. But for people who don't know C-3PO, his principal role is protocol and etiquette. Now, if there are two things that never exist in the *Star Wars* galaxy it's protocol and etiquette. He was programmed to make people feel comfortable and for them to make other people feel comfortable. So, for the most part, he's horrified by what he sees going on around him. He abhors space travel; he hates battles, and he hates drama. He just wants to be serving the canapés and the cocktails. I think why people relate to C-3PO is because they recognize themselves in him. He can be overt about something he doesn't like, and he can say he wants to go home."

One of the delights of returning to *Star Wars* for Daniels was reuniting with old friends from the cast of the original movies, both on set and off. "Back in 1977, I'd take Mark [Hamill], Carrie [Fisher], and Harrison [Ford] to the local Indian restaurant in London. The other night, there we were bowling, in a bowling alley, with Carrie! Tonight, I'm off with Mark and his family to a fish and chip shop!" the actor laughed. "That's the normalcy: You can do wacky stuff in the day, then you do fish and chips. Being in scenes with these characters just feels right. I was doing a scene with Carrie the other day, and during rehearsal I looked straight into her eyes, her beautiful eyes, and she looked straight back into my bloodshot ones, and we had total understanding of what we were talking about. It must be difficult for her and the others, that when I put the

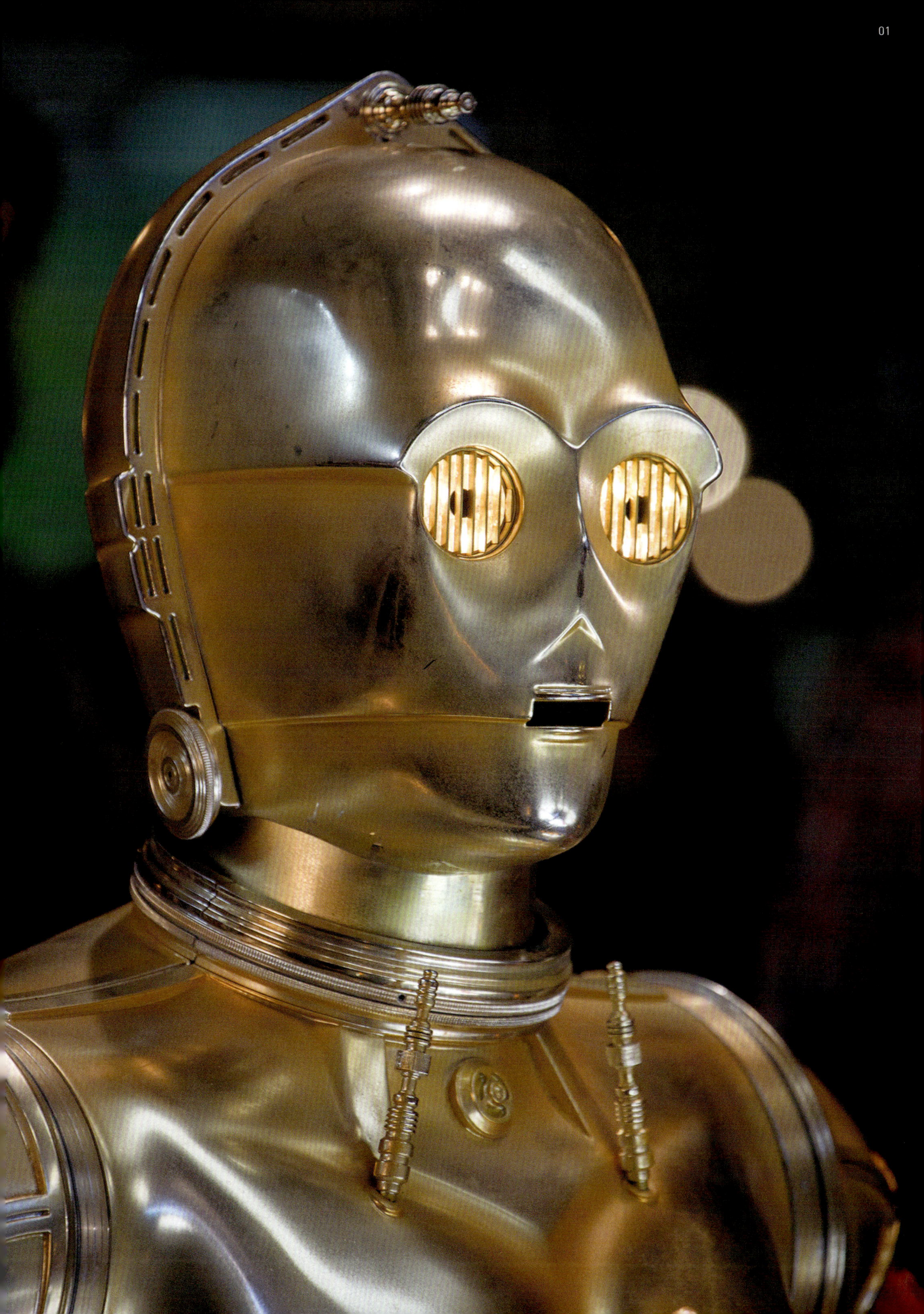

03

face on they're looking at this gold mask. They have to look straight into that and hopefully remember the emotion that they'd seen on my face. If C-3PO is worried, I'm worried. I've said that one of the reasons C-3PO works is the reflected reality of the other actors. If they walk on and working with a gold man doesn't make sense to them, the audience wouldn't believe it either. But their belief passes through their faces to you as a member of the audience. So, to see Carrie looking with great sincerity, and talking with great sincerity, to C-3PO is a joy. I think she's very fond of him too. They've been together a long time."

While time had moved on in the galaxy far, far away by the time of *The Force Awakens*, C-3PO remained pretty much unchanged. "There are tiny nuances that are different," Daniels revealed. "Some of them are technical on the inside, and that's for me to know. But there are other little additions, and fans will enjoy that. In *A New Hope*, C-3PO's left leg was silver, and nobody ever noticed because it was light silver, which would merely reflect the gold or the desert or the sand. George Lucas' original idea was that C-3PO had a history. The idea that *Star Wars* didn't just happen out of nowhere; it wasn't page one of a story. It was page a million of an age-old story of good and evil. One of George's concepts was that characters should be broken down, used, scratched, to make you think something has happened in the past. Move forward and J.J. Abrams has taken that idea several notches higher. C-3PO (and I don't know how he feels about it, but I don't think he'd be happy about it because he is a purist) has a red arm. His left arm is a fairly brutal, red, rusty, sanguine thing. Something has happened to him in the last 30 years. The rebels have had all sorts of dramas, and one of his was clearly losing a limb. In Episode VIII or by Episode IX, it would be nice to be back in one piece!"

04

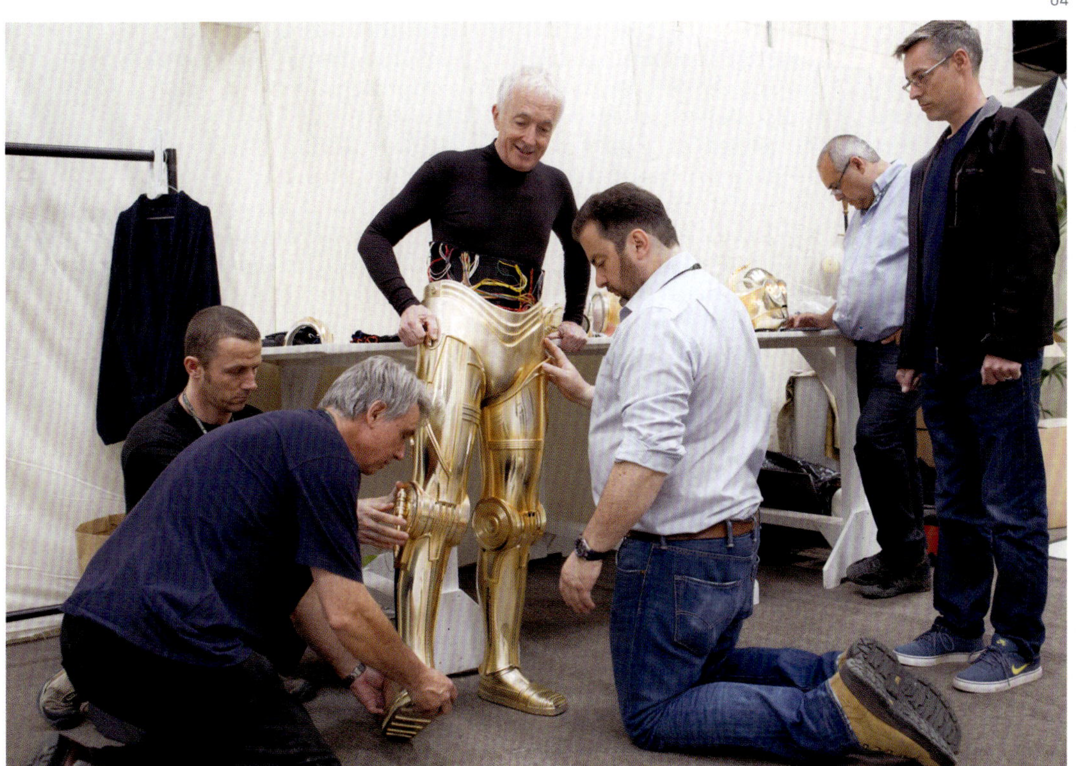

01 Previous page: Anthony Daniels as C-3PO.

02 The *Star Wars* saga's most dependable droids finally reunited.

03 Daniels rehearsing as C-3PO on location at RAF Greenham Common.

04 Several technical improvements were made to Daniels' new C-3PO costume, along with more visual nuances such as his red arm.

# RETURN OF THE WOOKIEE

## PETER MAYHEW & JOONAS SUOTAMO: CHEWBACCA

The friendship between Chewbacca and Han Solo ran deeper than any life-debt the Wookiee felt he owed to the captain of the *Millennium Falcon*. The duo stuck together through thick and thin, even when their credit in the galaxy was at its lowest. Then war returned, and once again they found themselves on the frontline.

Peter Mayhew first became an actor when he played the Minotaur in *Sinbad and the Eye of the Tiger* (1977). "That was a wonderful opportunity," remembered the actor. "About six months later, I got a phone call that they were looking for a tall person for another movie. That led to an interview with George Lucas. George's office was enormous. I sat down on the sofa and when George walked in, I stood up. The interview was just about over at that point. We went down to the creature shop and got a face mask done. The next day we went to a costume shop in London and got the suit made. Everything started to happen from that point on. It was a remarkable time in my life."

Mayhew went on to play Chewbacca throughout the original trilogy and reprised the role for 2005's *Star Wars: Revenge of the Sith*. When rumors began circulating almost a decade later that a new sequel was in the works, the actor crossed his fingers and hoped he might be involved. "It was just a question of waiting and seeing what was happening, and whether it would be a series or just one movie," recalled the actor. "At that stage, I wasn't walking very well. I'd torn a tendon in my knee and wound up having both knees replaced. It took time to get kneecaps that would fit me, and I wasn't sure I would be able to walk well enough to make the film, which by then I had learned was actually going to happen. But I wanted to do it."

Thankfully Mayhew was in good shape by the time filming commenced and found himself once again being fitted for a Chewbacca costume. "It was a completely new suit, but it looked as good as the original," he recalled. "It was built the same way, with all the fur sewn in—the yak hair stuff that they used for the old costume—but it was better. It was lighter."

Stepping back onto the *Millennium Falcon* was a prospect Mayhew tried not to think about too much beforehand, although J.J. Abrams had assured him that it was going to be good. "I decided not to be too over-enthusiastic," Mayhew admitted. In the event, the new set turned out to be incredibly accurate to the original, as Mayhew recalled, "There were only two levers that actually worked— and there were only two in the old set too!"

Due to his mobility issues, Mayhew shared the role of Chewbacca in *The Force Awakens* with former professional basketball player Joonas Suotamo, who played the character in more physically demanding scenes.

"*Star Wars* films were the first movies that I really remember watching," recalled Joonas Suotamo. "I didn't really realize there was a man inside Chewbacca. I remember thinking that he was just a bear that they found somewhere."

02

03

04

05

Suotamo was chosen to be the "bear" for a new generation of fans after nearly five months of auditions for a project called "Foodles"—a working alias for *The Force Awakens*. The process began with him sending a video, filmed by his girlfriend, of his best impression of a caveman. Almost half a year later, following a trip to London to meet J.J. Abrams, he won the role of the world's favorite Wookiee.

"Before *The Force Awakens*, Peter [Mayhew] and I took part in what we called 'The Wookiee Bootcamp,'" revealed Suotamo. "When we first met, he said I was a little bit too skinny! We spent a couple of weeks together, going into detail about how Peter used to make the suit work for him, the way, for example, that Chewbacca wears his chest proud. It was amazing to get that kind of detail, and I couldn't believe how gracious Peter was about it. I assured him that I had much respect for him and the character he made famous, so Chewie was going to be in good hands.

"Because of my love for *Star Wars* and all that comes with it, I wanted the Chewbacca that I played to be very similar in essence to the one that Peter played," he continued. "I wanted there to be that same feeling, when you look at this character, that he thinks about the same things that Peter thought about in the original trilogy."

The "walking carpet" Chewbacca costume was painstakingly recreated for the new movie, and it presented some challenges to Suotamo. "I did ask to see my scenes once we'd filmed them to be sure I'd done them justice. Being covered in hair, I didn't have the usual references that I would when working with my own face, and I wanted to do it well. So that's how I approached it."

Being "covered in hair" had other drawbacks, too, and Suotamo described these as the few "non-perks" of the job. "The suit required a lot of maintenance," he explained. "Hats off to everyone who worked on the suit after each day of sweat and whatever elements we were subjected to, because they had to take such good care of it! If I wanted to go to the bathroom, we'd have to remove the entire costume, which took about 10 minutes. Unfortunately, it takes longer than that to put it back on, but I wouldn't change it for the world."

01 Previous page: Peter Mayhew as Chewbacca.

02 Joonas Suotamo played Chewbacca in more physical sequences.

03 John Boyega (Finn) and Peter Mayhew (Chewbacca) enjoying a break in filming.

04 Animatronic designer Natalie Wickens at work on the Chewbacca mask.

05 Animatronic designer Emma Brassfield and supervising animatronics designer Maria Cork dress Peter Mayhew in his new Chewbacca costume.

# VILLAINS OF THE FIRST ORDER

Led by the terrifying Supreme Leader Snoke, the First Order rose from the ashes of the Galactic Empire, determined to gain absolute power and crush all resistance in its path. Actors Andy Serkis, Domhnall Gleeson, and Gwendoline Christie played a trio of its most powerful figures.

With Kylo Ren, played by Adam Driver, filling the position of *The Force Awaken*'s lead villain, it was down to three other actors to reveal the broader depth of the First Order's malevolence. Each character was strikingly different, visually; Supreme Leader Snoke appeared as a giant, seemingly omnipotent hologram; Captain Phasma was a faceless, chrome-plated enforcer; and General Armitage Hux was an uptight human in a military uniform. The actors therefore drew on different acting techniques to bring them to life.

With a résumé including roles such as Gollum in *The Lord of the Rings* trilogy, Captain Haddock in Steven Spielberg's *The Adventures of Tintin* (2011) and the title role in Peter Jackson's *King Kong* (2005), Andy Serkis has become known as one of cinema's leading motion-capture performers. In *The Force Awakens*, he took on the role of the shadowy Supreme Leader Snoke.

"Performance capture is the art and craft of an actor embodying a role that will be manifested on screen as a computer-generated character, but the authorship of the role, all the acting, takes place *with* other actors," explained Serkis during the movie's production. "Instead of putting on a costume and makeup beforehand, you're playing the role without the help of those things, but neither the hindrance. All of the facial expressions, all your acting decisions, happen on set with the other actors."

Snoke's threatening demeanor came directly from Serkis' acting choices, enhanced by the visual effects wizards of Industrial Light & Magic. "A clever team of animators and CG artists had the job of transposing the performance onto a digital avatar without losing the nuance and subtlety and underlying performance," said the actor. "Philosophically, it's the greatest acting tool of the 21st century. It doesn't matter what size you are. Stereotyping, or typecasting, is dead. It doesn't matter what the color of your skin or your height or your sex is. It's a brilliantly liberating tool that actors are finally seeing, and the more it's used as a standard industry tool, it's really proliferated."

01

01 Andy Serkis performing as Snoke in full motion-capture gear.

02 Supreme Leader Snoke. Concept art by Ivan Manzella.

02

03

04

05

03 Gwendoline Christie as Captain Phasma.

04 Phasma (Christie) and General Hux (Gleeson).

05 Christie rehearses a shot with J.J. Abrams for the opening scenes of the movie.

06 Costume concept designer Dermot Power's art of a cloaked stormtrooper became Captain Phasma.

For Gwendoline Christie the challenge was quite different, bringing life to the character of Captain Phasma from beneath an all-encompassing shell of chrome armor.

"The costume was absolutely sensational," recalled Christie. "From the second I put [it] on, I really felt like I wanted to have some fun with it. I wanted the character to have femininity and a heavy dose of sass, because I don't think we've seen that in a stormtrooper before. It certainly made me stand up straight. That glorious, majestic helmet, whose edges looked as if they could cut you like a knife."

Christie had no concerns about performing as a masked character, as she'd trained in classical acting techniques at drama school, including Lecoq mime and physical theatre that incorporated mask work. "I felt as if I could get away with a lot more than when my own dear face is exposed. When I put the helmet on, I felt like I could probably get away with blue murder," the actor joked. "There is something irresistible about Captain Phasma, [although] I think it might be in the costume rather than me. I think it's forward-thinking and modern for *Star Wars* to have that kind of character archetype and to investigate that side of femininity."

07

08

09

07 Gleeson (left) and Christie (right) on the Starkiller Base set.

08 Adam Driver (Kylo Ren), Domhnall Gleeson (Hux), and Gwendoline Christie (Phasma) filming a scene on the Star Destroyer bridge.

09 Gleeson as Hux on the partial set of Snoke's holographic chamber.

10 Domhnall Gleeson as General Hux.

Irish actor Domhnall Gleeson played the villainous General Hux, a more familiar *Star Wars* bad guy with his fascistic uniform and clipped British accent. "He isn't a particularly nice fella!" Gleeson said of the character.

Hux's First Order uniform was created by costume designer Michael Kaplan, who looked back to the Imperial uniforms of the original trilogy for inspiration. "Michael did an amazing job. It absolutely feels like *Star Wars*," said Gleeson. "You immediately recognize the world, but it's also slightly different than what they did before. Hux had to carry an aura of power and a preoccupation of being in charge of things. The clothes corrected [my] posture, so [it was] brilliant and hilarious to put them on every morning."

The tangible nature of the costumes, sets, and props were additional tools that enabled Gleeson to bring truth to his portrayal. "I was able to reach out and touch everything. Everything was right in front of you, which just makes acting so much easier," the actor said. "For me, just walking around and seeing all that stuff and putting my hands on it, and it being tactile and present, it was the stuff you'd imagined when you were a kid. I know how lucky I was to be on sets like that. It was large-scale filmmaking that felt like a real story and not just effects. There was a real energy in the performances. This was *Star Wars*, and that required a step up."

# FOR THE RESISTANCE

An array of fascinating new characters stood alongside General Organa's Resistance against the rising tide of the First Order, played by actors including Max Von Sydow, Lupita Nyongo, and Greg Grunberg.

Born in Sweden in 1929, Max Von Sydow's impressive résumé included roles such as Jesus Christ in *The Greatest Story Ever Told* (1965) and Father Merrin in the horror classic *The Exorcist* (1973). Directed by *Star Wars: The Empire Strikes Back*'s Irvin Kershner in *Never Say Never Again* (playing James Bond's deadliest foe, Ernst Stavro Blofeld), Sydow was no stranger to science fiction and fantasy movies, with appearances as Judge Fargo in *Judge Dredd* (1995), Director Lamar Burgess in *Minority Report* (2003), and, most memorably, as Ming the Merciless in *Flash Gordon* (1980). Max Von Sydow's brief, but pivotal, role as the mysterious explorer Lor San Tekka kick-started the events of *The Force Awakens.*

"I've been a *Star Wars* fan from the beginning," the renowned actor revealed to *Star Wars Insider*. "I had a young boy at the time the first movie was released, which made it even more important."

Having been on many sets during his long and varied screen career, Sydow was impressed by the scale of a *Star Wars* production and how director J.J. Abrams managed to pull the movie off. "I was very impressed, because this film was an enormous piece of work," Sydow said. "Personally, I don't know how to make a film of this size, so I'm very impressed by somebody who can handle this kind of project and have a vision. Also, it's not just about *Star Wars*, it's not just about the adventure, it's also about a message. It's a message of enthusiasm, and also of wanting to put things right."

01

01 An old friend of General Leia Organa, Lor San Tekka (Sydow) provided Poe Dameron with crucial information as to the location of Luke Skywalker.

02 Max Von Sydow as Lor San Tekka.

02

Another member of movie's impressive global cast was Oscar-winner Lupita Nyongo, who donned a lycra bodysuit to motion-capture her performance as the digital character Maz Kanata.

"I grew up watching *Star Wars*. It used to come on TV on public holidays in Kenya," recalled Nyongo. "I loved it at the time, [although] I wasn't conscious of the kind of phenomenon it was. I loved it for what it was. I particularly loved R2-D2 and C-3PO, and, later, the Ewoks. It came to me at a time when everything on screen was real. It wasn't until I got involved that I realized what a cultural reference it is in America. It's everywhere!"

On a set filled with tangible props and animatronic creatures, Nyongo found it disconcerting but fun to be playing a character that would be realized via visual effects later. "Everything felt so real, and then there was me in this headcam, with lights shining in my face, walking around, covered in dots," she said. "It was all extremely new to me. I had no idea what the motion capture suit would look like, or the dots that would be required on my face. I did not know any of that."

Nyongo embraced this new way of performing, learning on the job. "It is quite a fascinating process. The number of people behind [Maz Kanata] was just spellbinding. And they all knew what *they* were doing. My responsibility was to remain true to the character," she said. "Principal photography for me was more of a technical rehearsal. There was [then] a whole other process where we zeroed in on my performance and got the nuances of that. It was incredible to have the opportunity to be on set with everyone else and feel what this world felt like before going into a more technical space."

03

04

05

06

03 Lupita Nyongo (right) on set with John Boyega and Joonas Suotamo as Chewbacca.

04 Maz Kanata was realized through a combination of CGI and Nyongo's motion-captured performance.

05 Lupita Nyongo.

06 Nyongo wearing her motion-capture costume.

07

08

07 Greg Grunberg as Temmin "Snap" Wexley.

08 "Snap" at the controls of a Resistance X-wing starfighter.

09 "Snap" (Grunberg, left) and Finn (John Boyega, right) during the Resistance briefing on D'Qar.

09

Temmin "Snap" Wexley, played by actor Greg Grunberg, heroically fought in the Battle of Starkiller Base, and the actor was more than happy to become part of *Star Wars* lore.

"I was absolutely blown away. I felt the same level of excitement that I did when I was 12 or 13, experiencing *Star Wars* for the first time," said Grunberg. "It was just like when you were a kid and you got to play pretend. It's been a while, in my acting career, since I've really felt that level of excitement toward something that was so familiar. Usually, it's a new role and something that I really have to think about how to approach. But this—I got to be a pilot in *Star Wars*!

More importantly, I knew I'd be doing this with my best friend [director J.J. Abrams]. Even before I knew I was going to be playing "Snap" Wexley, it was stunning to find out that J.J. was associated with something that meant so much to us growing up and shaped our tastes. For me, *Star Wars* was always an escape and such an incredibly deep, layered experience every time I watched the movie. Whether it was in the theater or at home, I would just get lost in it. To think that I would be able to contribute—even in the small way that I have—to such a huge saga, was just incredible."

Grunberg was especially thrilled to be working alongside some of his childhood idols.

"I got to be on set with *all* of my heroes!" the actor said. "I looked around and there was Harrison Ford, Carrie Fisher, and Anthony Daniels. After a couple of takes, J.J. came up to me and whispered into my ear, 'I can see you're watching the movie.' (*laughs*) My reactions weren't 'Snap' Wexley's, they were Greg Grunberg's reactions that had been building up for almost 40 years. It was like no other job I ever had or probably ever will have again."

# A FORCE REAWAKENED

Creature and special makeup effects supervisor Neal Scanlan came out of semi-retirement for *Star Wars: The Force Awakens*, bringing years of experience to the task of populating the reinvigorated galaxy with a wealth of beings and droids.

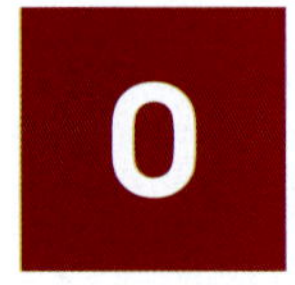

One of the founding members of Jim Henson's Creature Shop in London, Neal Scanlan had been working in film and television effects for 30 years when he decided to close down his own effects company in 2011, having decided to move on from the movie business to explore other avenues of interest. However, just a few years later an opportunity came his way that the Oscar winning creature creator couldn't refuse.

"J.J. Abrams and Kathleen Kennedy had decided to shoot *Star Wars: The Force Awakens* in the U.K., so it was a case of me being in the right place at the right time," recalled Scanlan when *Insider* caught up with the effects artist in 2021. "Tommy Harper, who had worked with J.J. on *Star Trek* (2009), called me to ask if I'd be interested in meeting in London to discuss a project. He wouldn't tell me what it was, but we had a great meeting and a few weeks later I got a call asking if I'd meet J.J. Once we had had that meeting, I knew that we'd been awarded the film. And it was not just a relaunch of the *Star Wars* franchise, but also a relaunch for my career too."

Given the long history of *Star Wars*, it was a given that Scanlan and his team would be recreating some iconic species and droids for the new movie, but one of the major reasons he had been called upon to head-up *The Force Awakens* creature shop was his experience in generating new creatures.

"During pre-production, Tommy Harper asked me to come up with some ideas. We put a team together, and the happabore was one of the first things we started working on," said Scanlan. "My thinking was, how could we best demonstrate to J.J. and Kathy what was possible with animatronics, without getting into what people traditionally thought they were all about. I decided we should do the biggest thing we could and bring it to life by putting people inside it. That way there were no mechanics, just performers, so when J.J. walked onto the stage and this thing walked towards him, he could simply direct it. That felt like a good way of selling the philosophy of what we were going to do on the film."

Such practical creatures would often be seamlessly mixed with digital effects, and Scanlan was pragmatic in striking a balance between the two technologies.

"There is no merit in making things complicated," he said. "If we can put a puppeteer inside a creature, or on it, or against it, and use digital technology to assist that, then we've got something. On *The Force Awakens* we were relatively successful with our contributions to the film. They were very user friendly, and J.J. engaged very quickly with just how practical those practical effects could be."

01

02

Scanlan also had another group of experienced *Star Wars* effects artists to bring into play where necessary. "When we needed to, we had the genius of Industrial Light & Magic to step in and paint out any problems," he continued. "Roger Guyett, the visual effects supervisor, was the perfect partner. Roger could have easily said to J.J. 'Why don't we do BB-8 completely digitally throughout the film?' and J.J. could have said, 'You're completely right.' But that's not what he did. With ILM there's a maturity about giving work to practical teams.

"On a purely artistic level, nothing can be puppeteered as well as a person can do it. There's no robotic entity or computer program that can do what a person can do. Without the performance you just have a soulless thing, and in animatronics things can get in the way of translating that performance one hundred percent through to the puppet. Reducing it down to its most simplistic elements—the puppet and the performer, with as little as possible in the middle—you get the finest results."

An example of that was BB-8, who was primarily realized as a practical prop rather than a digital effect.

"BB-8 was by far the most difficult thing we had to do," said Scanlan. "It was a big challenge, not only getting to the point of knowing that working with puppeteers [Brian Herring and Dave Chapman] was the right way to go, but actually making the droid himself. Making a ball that's got things inside it and doesn't get scratched was phenomenally difficult. Josh Lee, our genius of an engineer, had to devise a way of creating his structure from the inside out. BB-8 was much more difficult than you'd think, and nothing

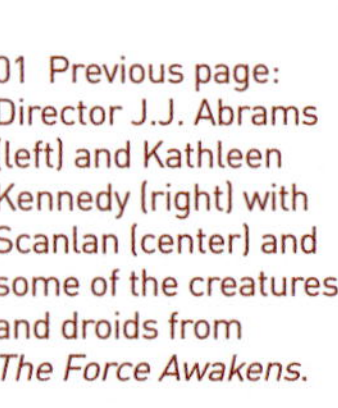

01 Previous page: Director J.J. Abrams (left) and Kathleen Kennedy (right) with Scanlan (center) and some of the creatures and droids from *The Force Awakens.*

02 Scanlan's team recreated several famous characters from the original trilogy for *The Force Awakens.*

03 The busy creature shop during the movie's pre-production phase.

04 Actor Simon Pegg trying the Unkar Plutt costume on for size.

03

04

06

like him had been done before. He tested all our departments."

Maz Kanata, on the other hand, was realized as an entirely digital character for *The Force Awakens*, using the motion-captured performance of Lupita Nyongo. "Maz was the character that wrung us out, creatively, on *The Force Awakens*. We just couldn't find her design, and the eureka moment didn't come until we'd almost finished filming," admitted Scanlan. "We always had a desire to do Maz as a puppet, and we were finally able to achieve that for *The Rise of Skywalker*."

Having returned to the film industry specifically for the opportunity to contribute to the *Star Wars* saga, Scanlan was happy to say he'd made a good decision.

"I've been the luckiest person in the industry. I don't know of any other person who's been as privileged as I am to come back into an industry and be given the opportunity to effectively start again," he said. "I was given the chance to say, 'If you could do this all over again, knowing what you now know, what would you do?' That's what the *Star Wars* films have done for me. They gave me that opportunity, and to be given that chance in the twilight years of your career is like being able to live my life again."

05 The life-sized happabore on location in Abu Dhabi.

06 Neal Scanlan adjusting a Bravaisian puppet on the set of Maz Kanata's castle.

# THE SAGA CONTINUES

*Star Wars: The Force Awakens* brought the saga back with a bang, but it was just the beginning of a new era for the venerable space fantasy. Two more sequels would follow to close out the Skywalker saga, and there were plenty of other *Star Wars* stories about to be told.

The theatrical release of *The Force Awakens* was supported by a publishing initiative that provided further storytelling expanding on plot points from the movie, under the banner *Journey to The Force Awakens*.

Leading the charge were two novels. Chuck Wendig's *Star Wars: Aftermath* (the first of a trilogy) chronicled the final battles of the Galactic Civil War following the Battle of Endor, while Claudia Grays' *Star Wars: Lost Stars* was a romance that led readers into the heart of the Battle of Jakku, revealing how the desert planet became the wreckage-strewn wasteland seen in the movie. Several short stories (eventually reprinted in the film's novelization) and a Marvel Comics four-part mini-series, written by Greg Rucka and entitled *Shattered Empire*, were also published, as was *Before the Awakening*, an anthology also written by Rucka that focused on the experiences of Rey, Finn, and Poe Dameron prior to the events of the movie.

But this was merely the beginning, as already another *Star Wars* project had begun principal photography at Pinewood Studios in England on August 8, 2015, a full four months before *The Force Awakens* was unleashed—and it wasn't Episode VIII.

Based on an idea devised by Industrial Light & Magic visual effects artist John Knoll, *Rogue One: A Star Wars Story* took the saga full circle to reveal how the Rebel Alliance secured the plans to the Empire's Death Star and ending moments before the opening scene of *Star Wars: A New Hope*. The film was released in cinemas across the globe on December 16, 2016, almost a year to the day after *The Force Awakens*. It was a pattern that fans would become accustomed to over the following few years.

Pinewood Studios continued to be the home of the saga when director Rian Johnson and the cast and crew for *Star Wars: The Last Jedi* took up residence in February 2016. Luke Skywalker, played once again by Mark Hamill, would this time play a prominent role as mentor to Rey as she began her training in the Force. John Boyega's Finn and Oscar Isaac's Poe Dameron had their own plot arcs to follow, and new characters were welcomed to the fold, including Kelly Marie Tran as Rose Tico, and Laura Dern as Vice Admiral Amilyn Holdo. The film featured a greatly expanded role for Andy Serkis as Supreme Leader Snoke, and Benicio Del Toro gave a salubrious performance as tech slicer DJ.

02

01 Previous page: The promotional poster for the first season of *Star Wars Resistance*.

02 Kylo Ren made a guest appearance in *Resistance*'s second season, voiced by Matthew Wood.

03 Season 2 saw the conflict with the First Order impact upon the residents of the *Colossus*.

04 The Skywalker saga ended with *Star Wars: The Rise of Skywalker*.

04 *Star Wars: The Mandalorian*.

Meanwhile, animated series *Star Wars Rebels* continued to thrill television audiences, with its second season airing as *The Force Awakens* arrived in cinemas. After the series ended in 2018, a new show set during the First Order era followed, designed to bridge the time between *The Last Jedi* and the final film in the sequel trilogy, *Star Wars: The Rise of Skywalker*. Across two seasons, *Star Wars Resistance* tied closely to the events of the sequel trilogy, often featuring guest appearances by Poe Dameron (voiced by Oscar Isaac), turning up to send the heroic Kaz Xiono (Christopher Sean) on another dangerous mission. The destruction of Hosnian Prime, as seen in *The Force Awakens*, was given a new perspective in the Season One climax, while the series finale—which aired a month after *The Rise of Skywalker* debuted in theaters—featured a cameo by Kylo Ren, voiced by Matthew Wood, who played General Grievous in *Star Wars: Revenge of the Sith*.

The sequel trilogy ended with the release of *The Rise of Skywalker* on December 19, 2019. By this time, the focus for *Star Wars* had moved to Disney+, where *The Mandalorian* became the first live-action television iteration of the space fantasy, set in a time period between the original and sequel trilogies that had yet to be explored.

At *Star Wars Celebration* Japan, 2025, fans learned the title of a new movie—*Star Wars: Starfighter*—that would take place beyond the events of the sequel trilogy and into a new era of *Star Wars* storytelling.

03

04

05

# STAR WARS LIBRARY

STAR WARS: THE MANDALORIAN GUIDE TO SEASON TWO

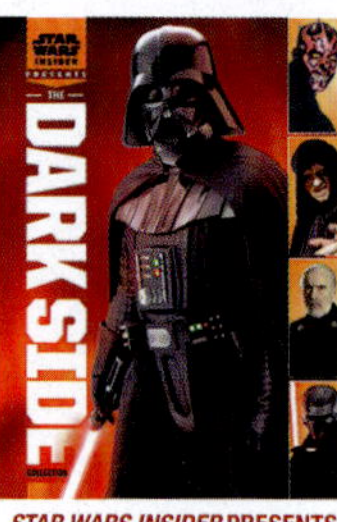
STAR WARS INSIDER PRESENTS THE DARK SIDE COLLECTION

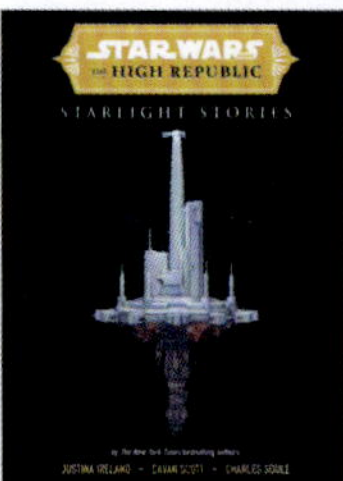
STAR WARS THE HIGH REPUBLIC STARLIGHT STORIES

STAR WARS THE HIGH REPUBLIC TALES OF ENLIGHTENMENT

STAR WARS: THE RETURN OF THE JEDI 40TH ANNIVERSARY SPECIAL

STAR WARS: THE PHANTOM MENACE 25TH ANNIVERSARY SPECIAL

STAR WARS: REVENGE OF THE SITH 20TH ANNIVERSARY SPECIAL

- ROGUE ONE: A STAR WARS STORY THE OFFICIAL COLLECTOR'S EDITION
- ROGUE ONE: A STAR WARS STORY THE OFFICIAL MISSION DEBRIEF
- STAR WARS: THE LAST JEDI THE OFFICIAL COLLECTOR'S EDITION
- STAR WARS: THE LAST JEDI THE OFFICIAL MOVIE COMPANION
- STAR WARS: THE LAST JEDI THE ULTIMATE GUIDE
- SOLO: A STAR WARS STORY THE OFFICIAL COLLECTOR'S EDITION
- SOLO: A STAR WARS STORY THE ULTIMATE GUIDE
- THE BEST OF STAR WARS INSIDER VOLUME 1
- THE BEST OF STAR WARS INSIDER VOLUME 2
- THE BEST OF STAR WARS INSIDER VOLUME 3
- THE BEST OF STAR WARS INSIDER VOLUME 4
- STAR WARS: LORDS OF THE SITH
- STAR WARS: HEROES OF THE FORCE
- STAR WARS: ICONS OF THE GALAXY
- STAR WARS: THE SAGA BEGINS
- STAR WARS THE ORIGINAL TRILOGY
- STAR WARS: ROGUES, SCOUNDRELS AND BOUNTY HUNTERS
- STAR WARS: CREATURES, ALIENS, AND DROIDS
- STAR WARS: THE RISE OF SKYWALKER THE OFFICIAL COLLECTOR'S EDITION
- STAR WARS: THE MANDALORIAN: GUIDE TO SEASON ONE
- STAR WARS: THE MANDALORIAN: GUIDE TO SEASON TWO
- STAR WARS: THE EMPIRE STRIKES BACK THE 40TH ANNIVERSARY SPECIAL EDITION
- STAR WARS: AGE OF RESISTANCE THE OFFICIAL COLLECTOR'S EDITION
- STAR WARS: THE SKYWALKER SAGA THE OFFICIAL COLLECTOR'S EDITION
- STAR WARS INSIDER: FICTION COLLECTION VOLUME 1
- STAR WARS INSIDER: FICTION COLLECTION VOLUME 2
- STAR WARS INSIDER PRESENTS: MANDALORIAN SEASON 2 VOLUME 1
- STAR WARS INSIDER PRESENTS: MANDALORIAN SEASON 2 VOLUME 2

# MARVEL STUDIOS LIBRARY

**MOVIE SPECIALS**

- MARVEL STUDIOS' SPIDER-MAN FAR FROM HOME
- MARVEL STUDIOS' ANT-MAN AND THE WASP
- MARVEL STUDIOS' AVENGERS: ENDGAME
- MARVEL STUDIOS' AVENGERS: INFINITY WAR
- MARVEL STUDIOS' BLACK PANTHER (COMPANION)
- MARVEL STUDIOS' BLACK WIDOW
- MARVEL STUDIOS' CAPTAIN MARVEL
- MARVEL STUDIOS: THE FIRST TEN YEARS
- MARVEL STUDIOS' THOR: RAGNAROK
- MARVEL STUDIOS' AVENGERS: AN INSIDER'S GUIDE TO THE AVENGERS' FILMS
- MARVEL STUDIOS' WANDAVISION
- MARVEL STUDIOS' THE FALCON AND THE WINTER SOLDIER
- MARVEL STUDIOS' LOKI
- MARVEL STUDIOS' ETERNALS
- MARVEL STUDIOS' HAWKEYE
- MARVEL STUDIOS' SPIDER-MAN: NO WAY HOME

MARVEL STUDIOS' DOCTOR STRANGE IN THE MULTIVERSE OF MADNESS THE OFFICIAL MOVIE SPECIAL

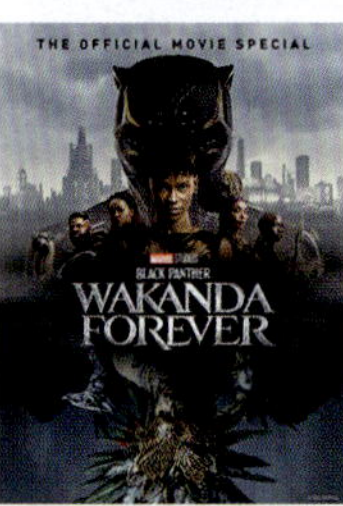
MARVEL STUDIOS' PANTHER WAKANDA FOREVER THE OFFICIAL MOVIE SPECIAL

MARVEL STUDIOS' THOR: LOVE AND THUNDER THE OFFICIAL MOVIE SPECIAL

SPIDER-MAN ACROSS THE SPIDER-VERSE THE OFFICIAL MOVIE SPECIAL

# MARVEL LEGACY LIBRARY

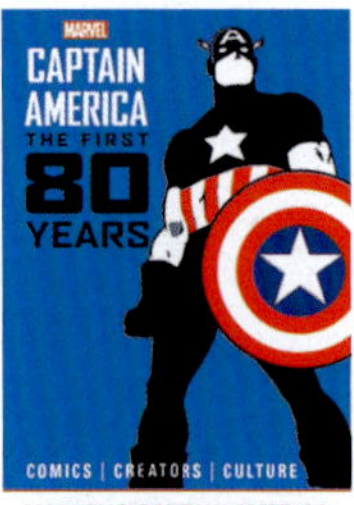
MARVEL'S CAPTAIN AMERICA: THE FIRST 80 YEARS

MARVEL'S DAREDEVIL: THE FIRST 60 YEARS

MARVEL'S DEADPOOL: THE FIRST 60 YEARS

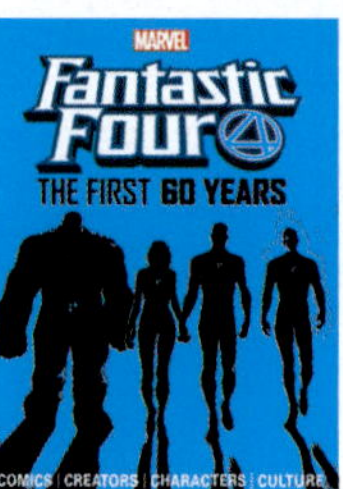
MARVEL'S FANTASTIC FOUR: THE FIRST 60 YEARS

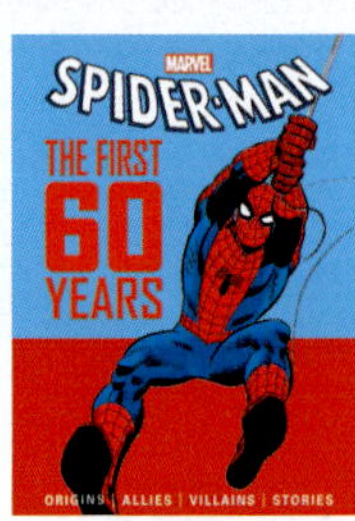
MARVEL'S SPIDER-MAN: THE FIRST 60 YEARS

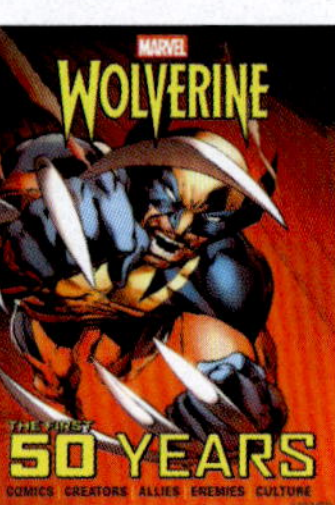
MARVEL'S WOLVERINE: THE FIRST 50 YEARS

MARVEL'S AVENGERS: THE FIRST 60 YEARS

**MARVEL CLASSIC NOVELS**

- WOLVERINE WEAPON X OMNIBUS
- SPIDER-MAN THE DARKEST HOURS OMNIBUS
- SPIDER-MAN THE VENOM FACTOR OMNIBUS
- X-MEN AND THE AVENGERS GAMMA QUEST OMNIBUS
- X-MEN MUTANT EMPIRE OMNIBUS

**NOVELS**

- MARVEL'S GUARDIANS OF THE GALAXY NO GUTS, NO GLORY
- SPIDER-MAN MILES MORALES WINGS OF FURY
- MORBIUS THE LIVING VAMPIRE: BLOOD TIES
- ANT-MAN NATURAL ENEMY
- AVENGERS EVERYBODY WANTS TO RULE THE WORLD
- AVENGERS INFINITY
- BLACK PANTHER WHO IS THE BLACK PANTHER?
- CAPTAIN AMERICA DARK DESIGNS
- CAPTAIN MARVEL LIBERATION RUN
- CIVIL WAR
- DEADPOOL PAWS
- SPIDER-MAN YOUNG
- SPIDER-MAN KRAVEN'S LAST HUNT
- THANOS DEATH SENTENCE
- VENOM LETHAL PROTECTOR
- X-MEN DAYS OF FUTURE PAST
- X-MEN THE DARK PHOENIX SAGA
- SPIDER-MAN HOSTILE TAKEOVER
- BLACK PANTHER: TALES OF WAKANDA
- BLACK PANTHER: PANTHER'S RAGE
- MARVEL'S ORIGINAL SIN
- MARVEL'S MIDNIGHT SUNS: INFERNAL RISING
- GUARDIANS OF THE GALAXY - ANNIHILATION: CONQUEST
- MARVEL'S SECRET INVASION
- CAPTAIN MARVEL: SHADOW CODE
- LOKI: JOURNEY INTO MYSTERY
- DOCTOR STRANGE: DIMENSION WAR

**ART BOOKS**

- MARVEL'S GUARDIANS OF THE GALAXY: THE ART OF THE GAME
- MARVEL'S AVENGERS: BLACK PANTHER: WAR FOR WAKANDA EXPANSION: ART OF THE HIDDEN KINGDOM
- MARVEL'S SPIDER-MAN: MILES MORALES – THE ART OF THE GAME
- MARVEL STUDIOS' THE INFINITY SAGA - THE AVENGERS: THE ART OF THE MOVIE
- MARVEL'S SPIDER-MAN THE ART OF THE GAME
- MARVEL CONTEST OF CHAMPIONS THE ART OF THE BATTLEREALM
- SPIDER-MAN: INTO THE SPIDER-VERSE THE ART OF THE MOVIE
- MARVEL STUDIOS' THE INFINITY SAGA - IRON MAN: THE ART OF THE MOVIE
- MARVEL STUDIOS' THE INFINITY SAGA - IRON MAN 2: THE ART OF THE MOVIE
- MARVEL STUDIOS' THE INFINITY SAGA - IRON MAN 3: THE ART OF THE MOVIE
- MARVEL STUDIOS' THE INFINITY SAGA - CAPTAIN AMERICA: THE WINTER SOLDIER: THE ART OF THE MOVIE
- MARVEL STUDIOS' THE INFINITY SAGA - THOR: THE ART OF THE MOVIE
- MARVEL STUDIOS' THE INFINITY SAGA - THOR: THE DARK WORLD: THE ART OF THE MOVIE
- MARVEL STUDIOS' THE INFINITY SAGA - CAPTAIN AMERICA: THE FIRST AVENGER: THE ART OF THE MOVIE

**AVAILABLE AT ALL GOOD BOOKSTORES AND ONLINE**

**TITAN**-COMICS.COM | **TITAN**BOOKS.COM